# FENCES

## AUTHENTIC DETAILS
### FOR
## DESIGN AND RESTORATION

PETER JOEL HARRISON

## JOHN WILEY & SONS, INC.
New York, Chichester, Weinheim, Brisbane, Singapore, Toronto

Harrison, Peter Joel.
    Fences : authentic details for design and restoration / Peter Joel
Harrison.
      p. cm.
    "Published simultaneously in Canada."
    Includes index.
    ISBN 0-471-32199-0 (cloth : alk. paper)
    1. Fences.    I. Title
NA8390.H275   1999
717--dc21                                           98-29321

Printed in the United States of America.

10 9 8 7 6 5 4

# TO THE READER.

I am very indebted to Mrs. Helen Mourton of Eastham and Mr. Peter S. MacGlashan of Nantucket for their fine efforts in showing me many wonderful fences and gates I surely would have missed without their aid. I am always eager for the help of knowledgeable people regarding these endeavors. So, I would ask if there are others who know of beautiful examples not yet recorded here, I would greatly welcome information concerning their whereabouts.

Thank you,

Peter Joel Harrison
2021 Fawndale Drive
Raleigh, North Carolina  27612

# TABLE OF CONTENTS.

PART I
## FENCES.

# PREFACE.

While visiting my father in North Carolina, my wife and I came upon a fine house that was for sale. It was seated upon a large piece of freshly cleared flat land. The house carpenter who built it showed us in. It was beautiful to behold.

When our visit was concluded, we began our journey back to New Jersey. My wife was unduly silent. As we crossed into Virginia, she began to weep and I was unable to stop her. She wanted that house more than breath. For she did not want to have a child reared in a tenement among scoundrels. As any good husband would, I made proper arrangements. Thus, we moved.

Once settled in, I found my first task was to enclose the yard. As I was duly proud of my new acquisition, I desired the fence to be of noble character. Thus, I went to bookshops to encourage my imagination, but found them wanting. The libraries and colleges also were barren. It became clear to me why the fences around me were so the same, there was not a pattern book.

Being an ambitious gentleman, I decided to search for myself the towns and countryside. For twelve years, as time permitted me, I made my journeys.

Now satisfied, I am pleased to say my land is nicely fenced with the finest pales and boards in the county.

With my mind and sketchbook filled, I have taken it upon myself to print the missing pattern book I once so eagerly looked for. Now after many years aforesaid, I lay open this work, for all those like myself engaged in the noble art of building.

Thank you,

Peter Joel Harrison

PART I

# FENCES

Moſt ELEGANT and USEFUL DESIGNS

*of*

# FENCES

In the Moſt FASHIONABLE TASTE.

| URNS | FINIALS |
|------|---------|
| BALLS | CAPS |

The Whole comprehended in NINETY-TWO PLATES, neatly drawn.

Calculated to improve and refine the preſent TASTE, of all
Perſons in all Degrees of Life.

# C H A P.  I.

## *Of* FENCE CONSTRUCTION

OF THE

# MAKING

*of*

# POSTS, RAILES & PALES.

POSTS ſhould be of ſound quality, ſeaſoned Stock of White Oak, Locuſt, or Cedar. Theſe ſhould be ſawn 4 Inches or 6 Inches Square, in a Length 7 Feet 6 Inches; the Foot of which ſhould be chared or tared before ſetting Poſts into Holes dug; the Holes of which ſhould be 2 Feet or 3 Feet in Depth and 8 Feet, 9 Feet, or 10 Feet apart. Stones may be used to wedge Poſts faſt.

Railes of White Oak, Poplar, or Pine ſhould be ſawn 2 Inches x 4 Inches, Mortiſed and Tennanted in Place and fixed with pegs.

Pales of Fir, Spruce, or Heart Pine cut 2 Inches or 2½ Inches in Breadth; 48 Inches in Length; 1 Inch thick; made ſmooth by a drawn Knife or Plane. Fix Pales to Railes 1 Inch to 2 Inches apart with Ten Penny Nailes.

*Plate 1.*

# Name Of The Members

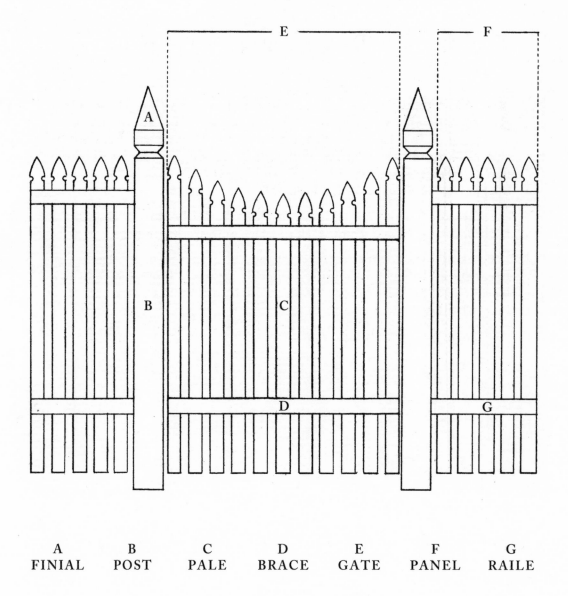

| A | B | C | D | E | F | G |
|---|---|---|---|---|---|---|
| FINIAL | POST | PALE | BRACE | GATE | PANEL | RAILE |

Plate 2.

# THE SCALE OF HEIGHTS & PROJECTIONS

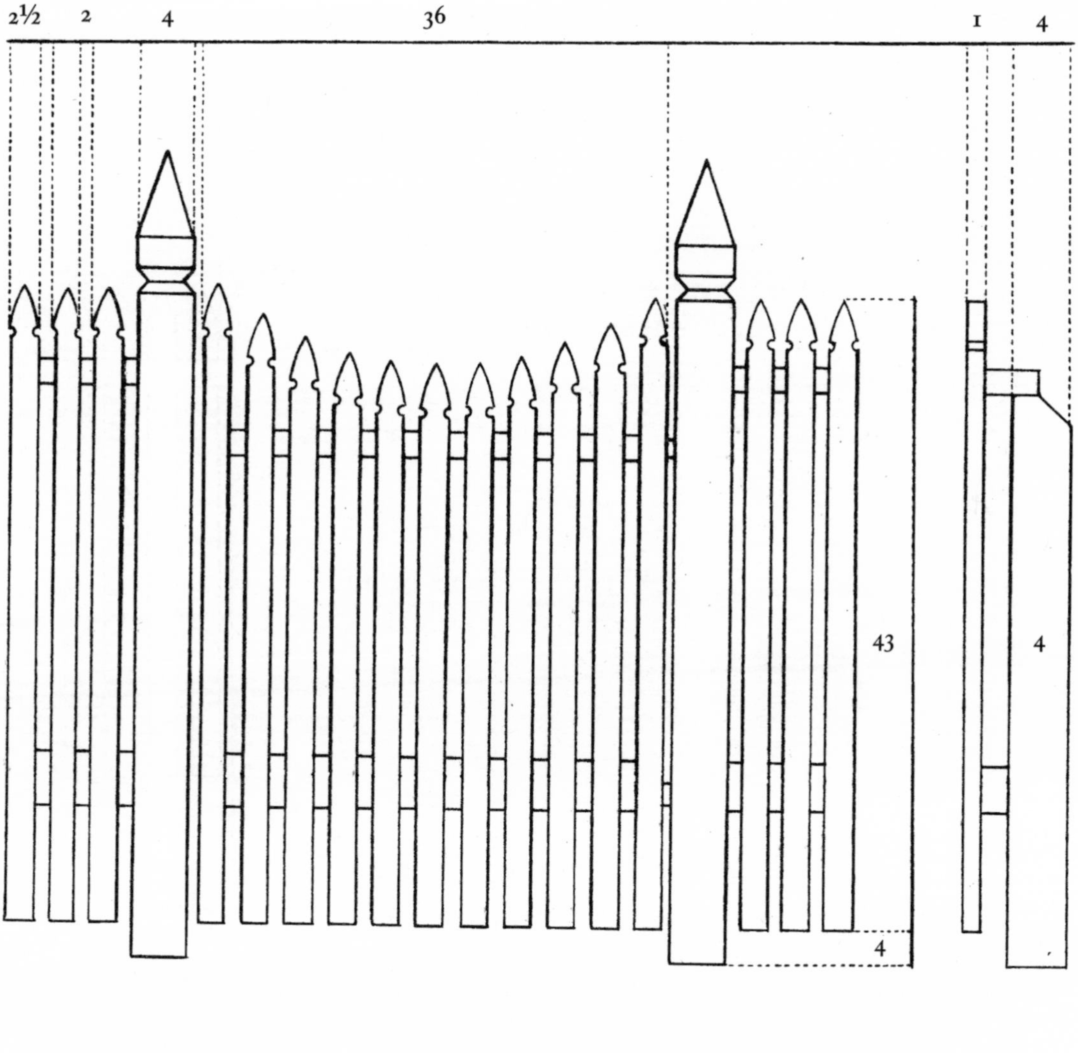

*FIG. 1.*

COLONIAL WILLIAMSBURG

Williamſburg, Virginia

*FIG. 2.*

COLONIAL WILLIAMSBURG

Williamſburg, Virginia

*FIG. 3.*

COLONIAL WILLIAMSBURG

Williamſburg, Virginia

*FIG. 4.*

THE PENDER MUSEUM

Tarboro, North Carolina

*Plate 3.*

# OF GATE BRACING

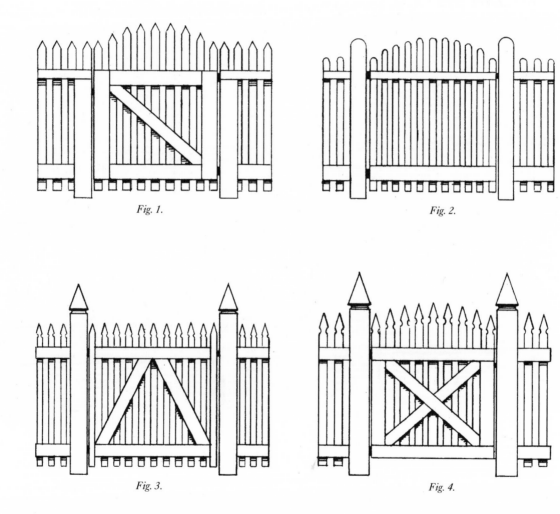

*Fig. 1.*

*Fig. 2.*

*Fig. 3.*

*Fig. 4.*

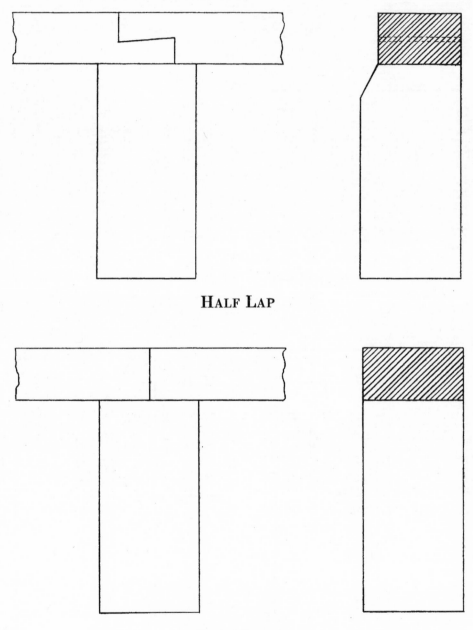

*Plate 4.*

# OF JOINTS FOR RAILES

HALF LAP

BUTT JOINT

Plate 5.

# OF JOINTS FOR RAILES

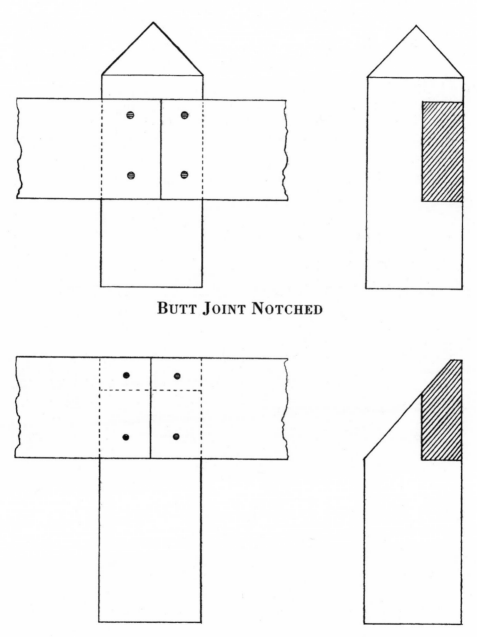

**BUTT JOINT NOTCHED**

**BUTT JOINT NOTCHED & SHAPED**

Plate 6.

# OF PANELS

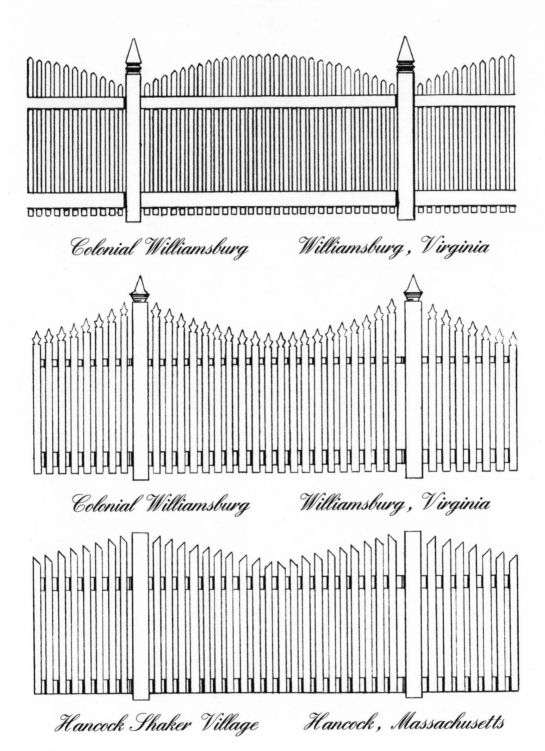

*Colonial Williamsburg*     *Williamsburg, Virginia*

*Colonial Williamsburg*     *Williamsburg, Virginia*

*Hancock Shaker Village*     *Hancock, Massachusetts*

# CHAP. II.
## *Of* POSTS

*FIG. 1.*

HOUSE-IN-THE-HORSESHOE

Carthage, North Carolina

*FIG. 2.*

OLD SALEM

Winston-Salem, North Carolina

*FIG. 3.*

COLONIAL WILLIAMSBURG

Williamſburg, Virginia

*FIG. 4.*

APPOMATTOX COURT HOUSE

Appomattox, Virginia

Plate 7.

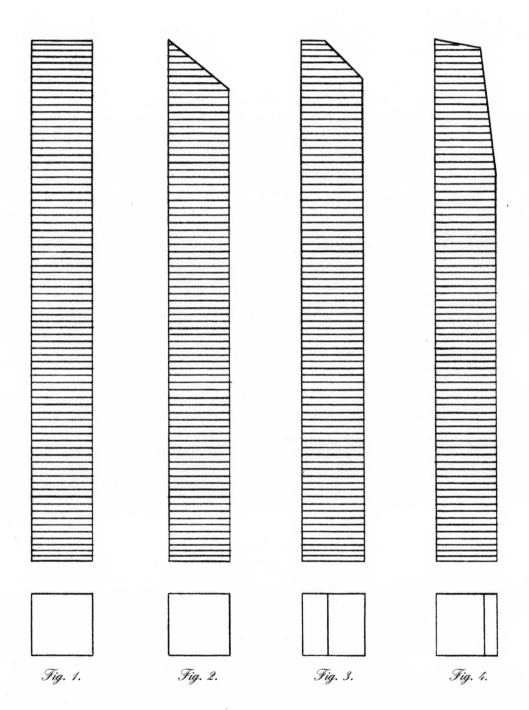

Fig. 1.                Fig. 2.                Fig. 3.                Fig. 4.

*FIG. 5.*
## OLD BETHPAGE VILLAGE
Bethpage, New York


*FIG. 6.*
## COLONIAL WILLIAMSBURG
Williamſburg, Virginia


*FIG. 7.*
## HOPE LODGE
Fort Waſhington, Pennſylvania


*FIG. 8.*
## PENNSBURY MANOR
Tullytown, Pennſylvania

Plate 8.

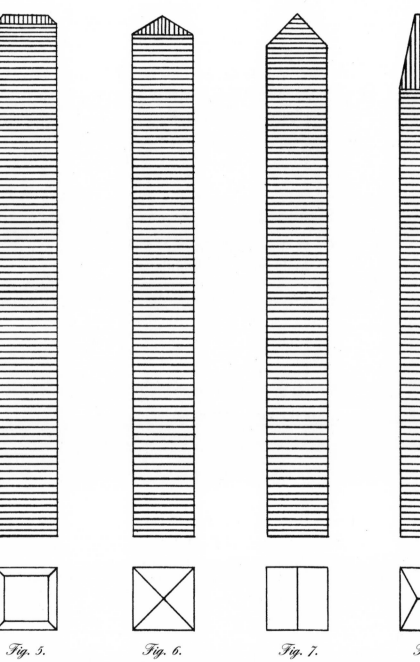

Fig. 5.          Fig. 6.          Fig. 7.          Fig. 8.

Plate 9.

Fig. 9.        Fig. 10.        Fig. 11.        Fig. 12.

*FIG. 13.*
## JOEL LANE HOUSE
Raleigh, North Carolina


*FIG. 14.*
## LIBERTY HALL
Kenanfville, North Carolina


*FIG. 15.*
## WOODLAWN PLANTATION
Mount Vernon, Virginia


*FIG. 16.*
## ADAM THOROUGHGOOD HOUSE
Virginia Beach, Virginia

Plate 10.

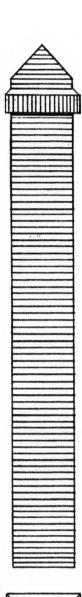

Fig. 13.          Fig. 14.          Fig. 15.          Fig. 16.

Plate 11.

# OF POSTS FOR COUNTER WEIGHTS

*Colonial Williamsburg*　　　*Williamsburg, Virginia*

*Plate 12.*

# OF POST & COUNTER WEIGHT FIXED

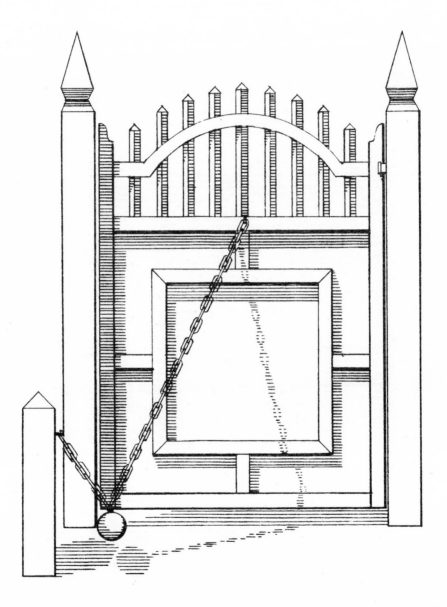

*St. James House          Fredericksburg, Virginia*

# C H A P.  I I I.
## *Of* PALES

*FIG. 1.*

New Hope, Pennſylvania


*FIG. 2.*

PENNSBURY MANOR

Tullytown, Pennſylvania


*FIG. 3.*

POTTSGROVE MANSION

Pottſtown, Pennſylvania


*FIG. 4.*

STRAWBERY BANKE

Portſmouth, New Hamſhire


*FIG. 5.*

PENNSBURY MANOR

Tullytown, Pennſylvania

Plate 13.

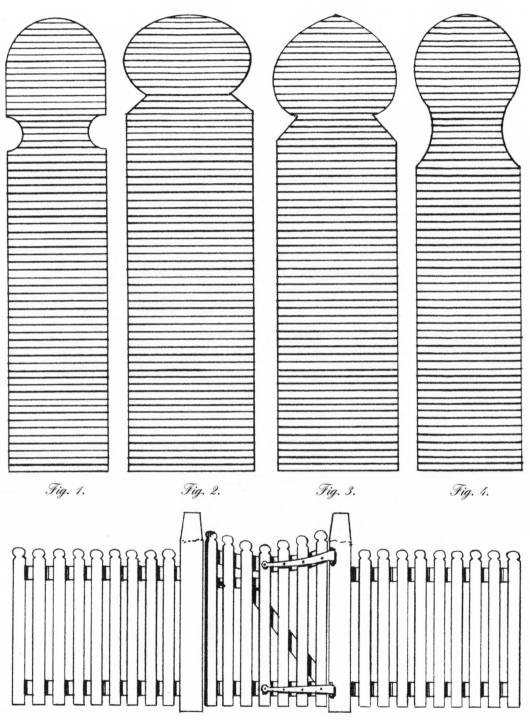

Fig. 1.      Fig. 2.      Fig. 3.      Fig. 4.

Fig. 5.

*FIG. 6.*

Savannah, Georgia


*FIG. 7.*

COLONIAL WILLIAMSBURG

Williamſburg, Virginia


*FIG. 8.*

MYSTIC SEAPORT

Myſtic, Connecticut


*FIG. 9.*

COLONIAL WILLIAMSBURG

Williamſburg, Virginia


*FIG. 10.*

MYSTIC SEAPORT

Myſtic, Connecticut


*FIG. 11.*

COLONIAL WILLIAMSBURG

Williamſburg, Virginia

Plate 14.

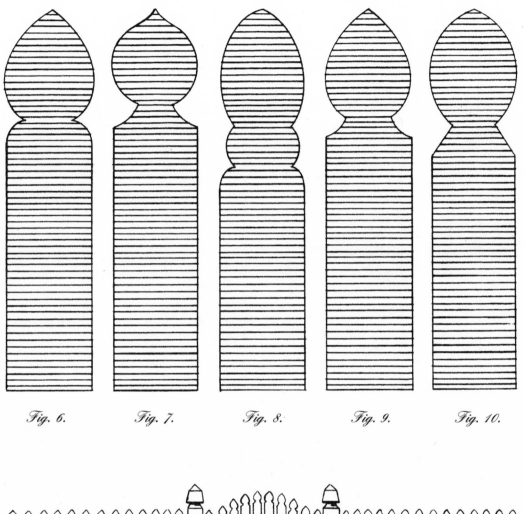

Fig. 6.     Fig. 7.     Fig. 8.     Fig. 9.     Fig. 10.

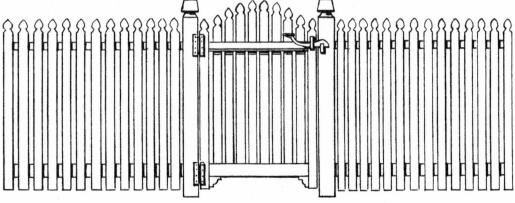

Fig. 11.

*FIG. 12.*

JULIA WOOD HOUSE

Falmouth, Maſſachuſetts

*FIG. 13.*

Odeſſa, Delaware

*FIG. 14.*

HILL HOLD

Montgomery, New York

*FIG. 15.*

MOUNT VERNON

Mount Vernon, Virginia

*FIG. 16.*

HILL HOLD

Montgomery, New York

Plate 15.

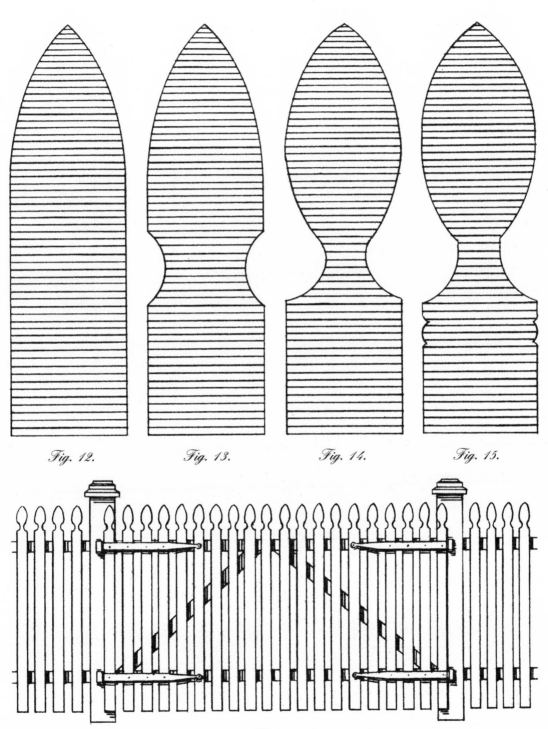

Fig. 12.     Fig. 13.     Fig. 14.     Fig. 15.

Fig. 16.

FIG. *17.*

MOUNT LEBANON SHAKER VILLAGE
New Lebanon, New York


FIG. *18.*

STEVENS-WEBB-DEANE HOUSE
Wethersfield, Connecticut


FIG. *19.*

WYCK
Philadelphia, Pennſylvania


FIG. *20.*

LOCUST LAWN
Gardiner, New York


FIG. *21.*

MOUNT LEBANON SHAKER VILLAGE
New Lebanon, New York

Plate 16.

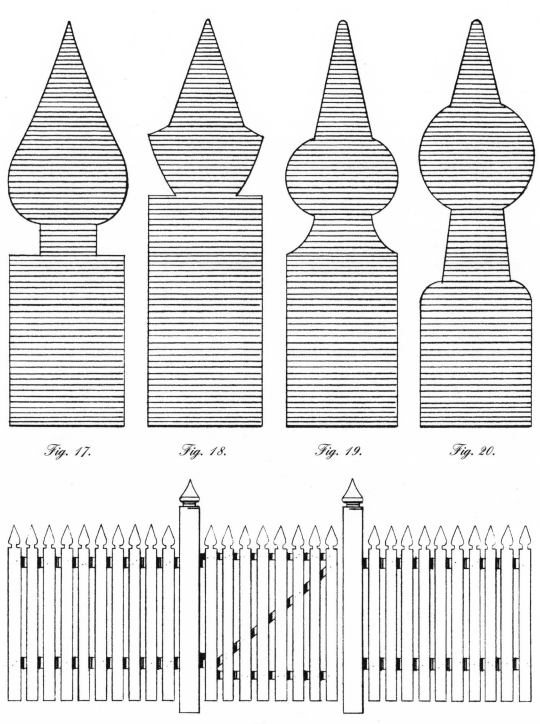

Fig. 17.    Fig. 18.    Fig. 19.    Fig. 20.

Fig. 21.

*FIG. 22.*

HOPE PLANTATION

Windſor, North Carolina

*FIG. 23.*

MOUNT VERNON

Mount Vernon, Virginia

*FIG. 24.*

APPOMATTOX COURT HOUSE

Appomattox, Virginia

*FIG. 25.*

COLONIAL WILLIAMSBURG

Williamſburg, Virginia

*FIG. 26.*

APPOMATTOX COURT HOUSE

Appomattox, Virginia

Plate 17.

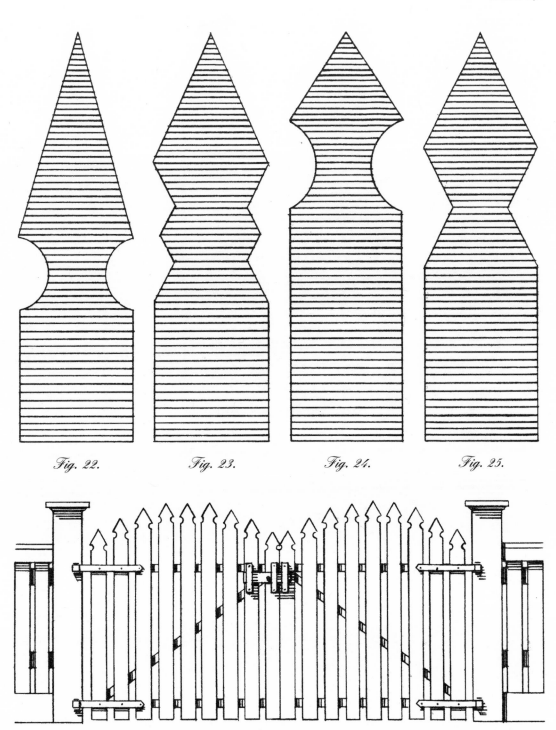

Fig. 22.     Fig. 23.     Fig. 24.     Fig. 25.

Fig. 26.

*FIG. 27.*

MOUNT VERNON

Mount Vernon, Virginia


*FIG. 28.*

LOCUST LAWN

Gardiner, New York


*FIG. 29.*

IREDELL HOUSE

Edenton, North Carolina


*FIG. 30.*

Clarkſville, Virginia


*FIG. 31.*

Clarkſville, Virginia

Plate 18.

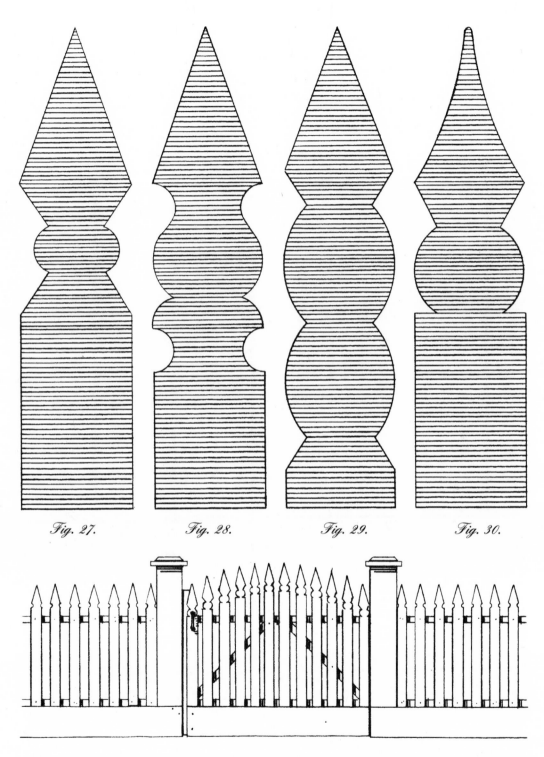

Fig. 27.          Fig. 28.          Fig. 29.          Fig. 30.

Fig. 31.

*FIG. 32.*

## COLONIAL WILLIAMSBURG
Williamſburg, Virginia


*FIG. 33.*

## COLONIAL WILLIAMSBURG
Williamſburg, Virginia


*FIG. 34.*

## COLONIAL WILLIAMSBURG
Williamſburg, Virginia


*FIG. 35.*

## PENDER MUSEUM
Tarboro, North Carolina


*FIG. 36.*

## PALMER-MARSH HOUSE
Bath, North Carolina


*FIG. 37.*

## COLONIAL WILLIAMSBURG
Williamſburg, Virginia

*Plate 19.*

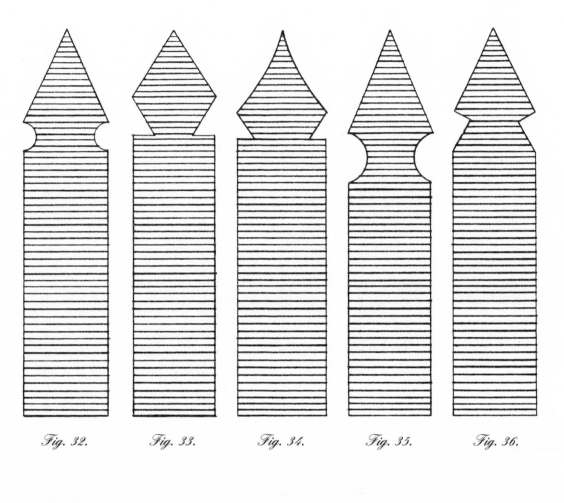

*Fig. 32.*          *Fig. 33.*          *Fig. 34.*          *Fig. 35.*          *Fig. 36.*

*Fig. 37.*

*FIG. 38.*

MARY BALL WASHINGTON HOUSE
Frederickſburg, Virginia


*FIG. 39.*

St. Mary's City, Maryland


*FIG. 40.*

SMITH'S FORT PLANTATION
Surry, Virginia


*FIG. 41.*

COLONIAL WILLIAMSBURG
Williamſburg, Virginia


*FIG. 42.*

SMITH'S FORT PLANTATION
Surry, Virginia

Plate 20.

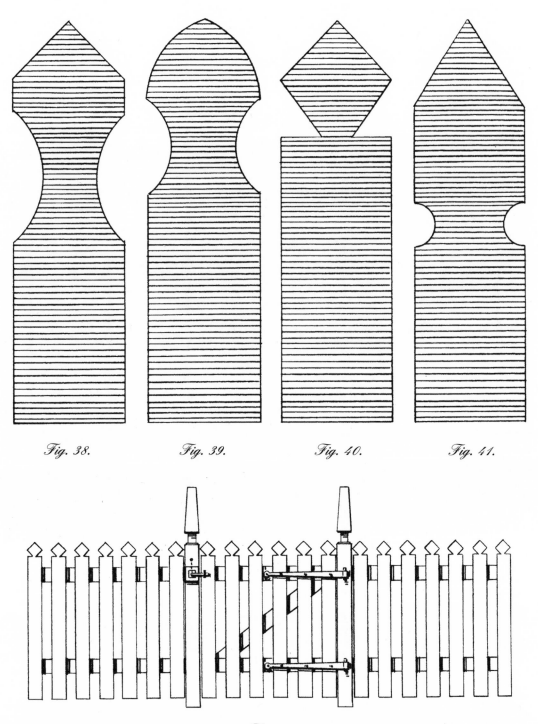

Fig. 38.  Fig. 39.  Fig. 40.  Fig. 41.

Fig. 42.

*FIG. 43.*
Newport, Rhode Ifland


*FIG. 44.*
LLOYD HOUSE
Alexandria, Virginia


*FIG. 45.*
Yorktown, Virginia


*FIG. 46.*
Frederickfburg, Virginia


*FIG. 47.*
Frederickfburg, Virginia

Plate 21.

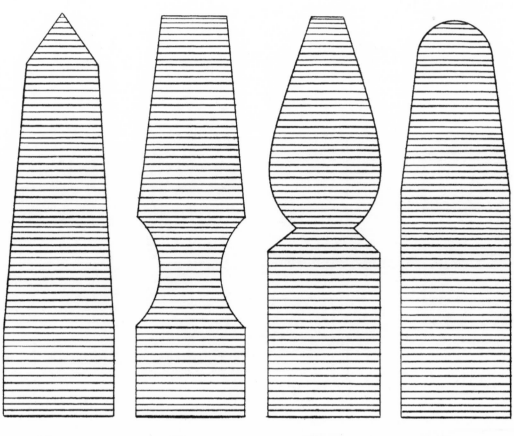

Fig. 43.        Fig. 44.        Fig. 45.        Fig. 46.

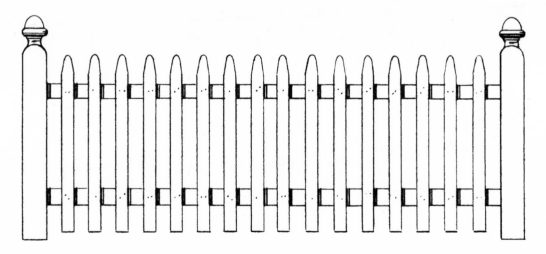

Fig. 47.

*FIG. 48.*

COLONIAL WILLIAMSBURG
Williamſburg, Virginia


*FIG. 49.*

COLONIAL WILLIAMSBURG
Williamſburg, Virginia


*FIG. 50.*

Newport, Rhode Iſland


*FIG. 51.*

OLD SALEM
Winſton-Salem, North Carolina


*FIG. 52.*

COLONIAL WILLIAMSBURG
Williamſburg, Virginia

Plate 22.

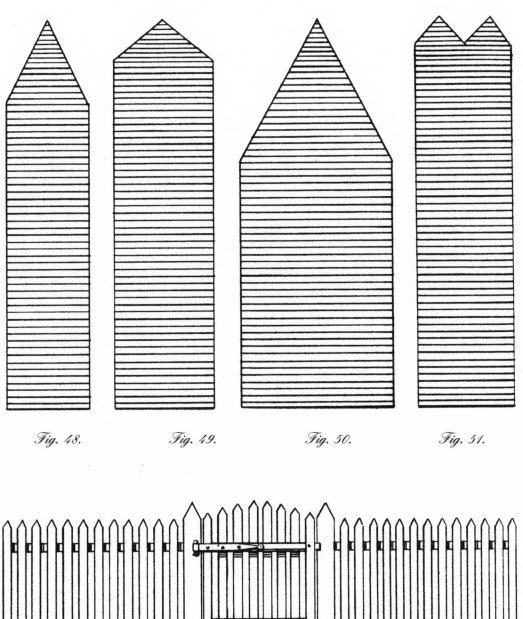

Fig. 48.     Fig. 49.     Fig. 50.     Fig. 51.

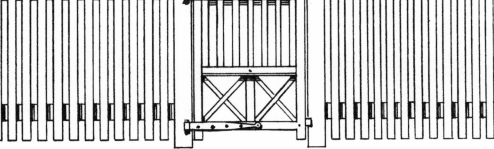

Fig. 52.

*FIG. 53.*
New Caftle, Delaware


*FIG. 54.*
COLONIAL WILLIAMSBURG
Williamfburg, Virginia


*FIG. 55.*
CUPOLA HOUSE
Edenton, North Carolina


*FIG. 56.*
COLONIAL WILLIAMSBURG
Williamfburg, Virginia

Plate 23.

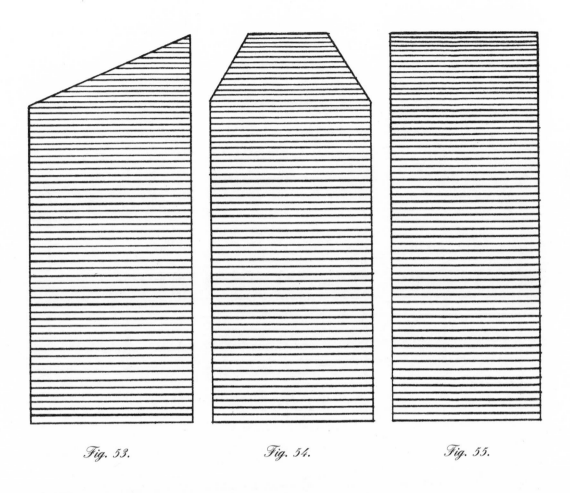

Fig. 53.          Fig. 54.          Fig. 55.

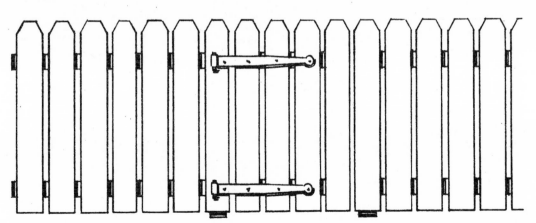

Fig. 56.

*FIG. 57.*

OLD SALEM

Winſton-Salem, North Carolina

*FIG. 58.*

COLONIAL WILLIAMSBURG

Williamſburg, Virginia

*FIG. 59.*

Odeſſa, Delaware

*FIG. 60.*

COLONIAL WILLIAMSBURG

Williamſburg, Virginia

Plate 24.

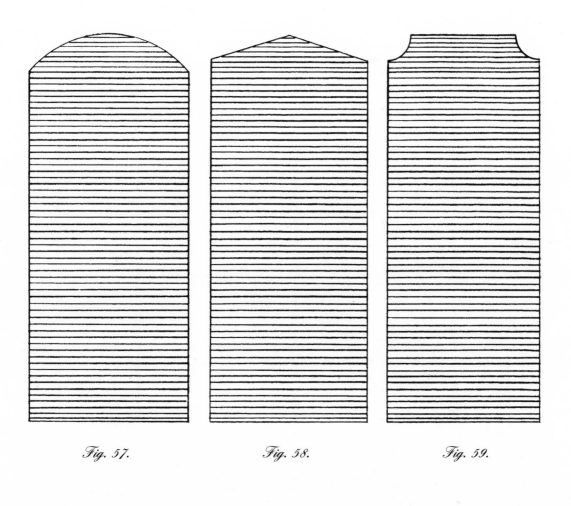

Fig. 57.          Fig. 58.          Fig. 59.

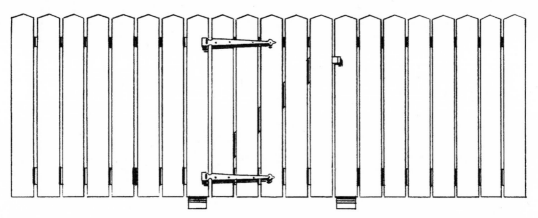

Fig. 60.

Plate 25.

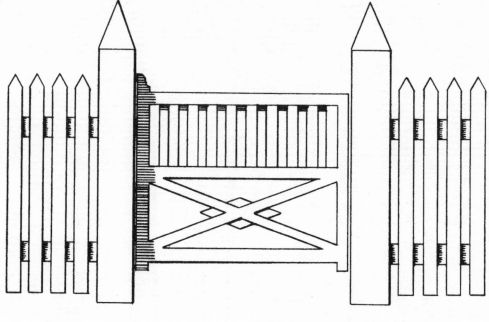

Colonial Williamsburg          Williamsburg, Virginia

*Plate 26.*

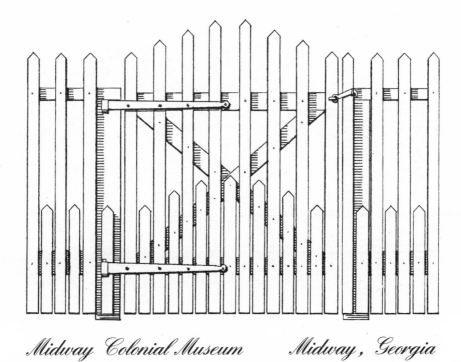

*Midway Colonial Museum      Midway, Georgia*

*Plate 27.*

*Cupola House     Edenton , North Carolina*

*Plate 28.*

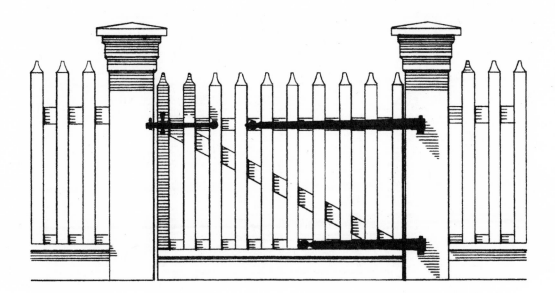

*South Dennis, New Jersey*

*Plate 29.*

*Colonial Williamsburg*       *Williamsburg, Virginia*

Plate 30.

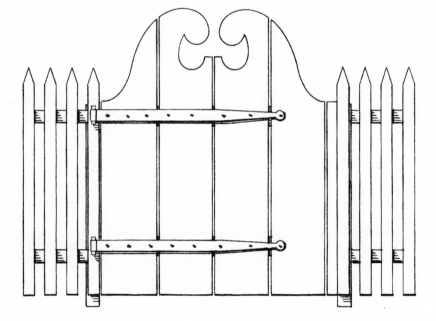

*Noah Webster House*        *West Hartford, Connecticut*

*Plate 31.*

*Stonington, Connecticut*

# CHAP. IV.

*Of* DOUBLE PALED & PICKET FENCES

*FIG. 1.*

# OLD STURBRIDGE VILLAGE
Sturbridge, Maſſachuſetts

*FIG. 2.*

# HOPSEWEE PLANTATION
Georgetown, South Carolina

*FIG. 3.*

# MYSTIC SEAPORT
Myſtic, Connecticut

*FIG. 4.*

# CHASE-LLOYD HOUSE
Annapolis, Maryland

*FIG. 5.*

# COLONIAL WILLIAMSBURG
Williamſburg, Virginia

Plate 32.

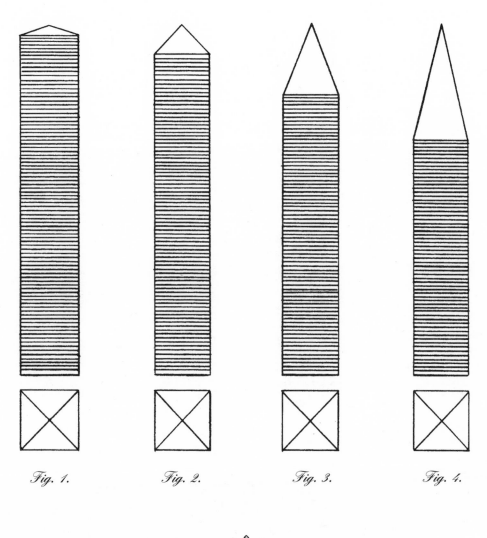

Fig. 1.        Fig. 2.        Fig. 3.        Fig. 4.

Fig. 5.

*Plate 33.*

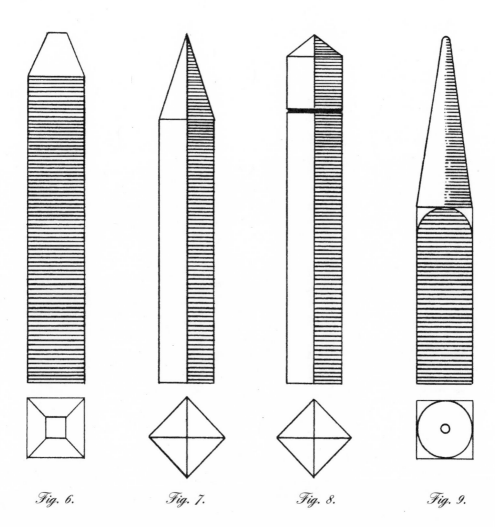

*Fig. 6.*     *Fig. 7.*     *Fig. 8.*     *Fig. 9.*

*Fig. 10.*

*FIG. 11.*

O L D   S A L E M
Winſton-Salem, North Carolina


*FIG. 12.*

Tarboro, North Carolina


*FIG. 13.*

Newport, Rhode Iſland


*FIG. 14.*

Newport, Rhode Iſland


*FIG. 15.*

O L D   S A L E M
Winſton-Salem, North Carolina

Plate 34.

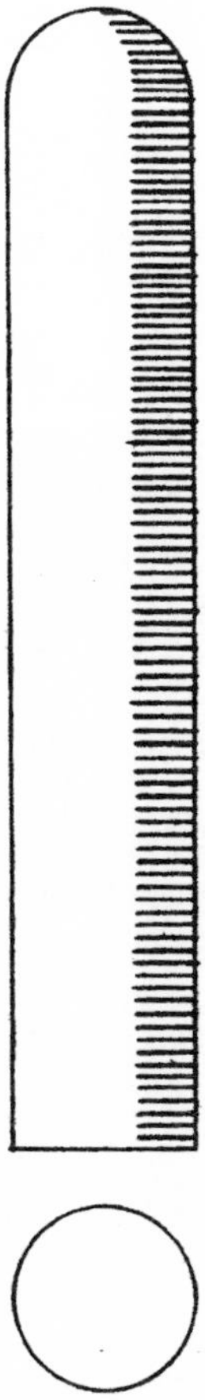

Fig. 11.

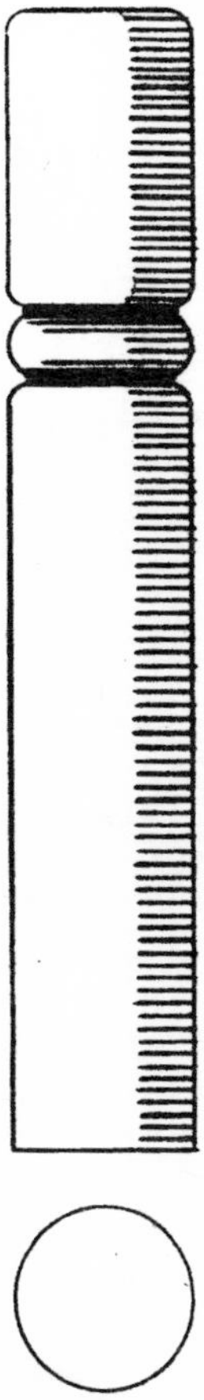

Fig. 12.

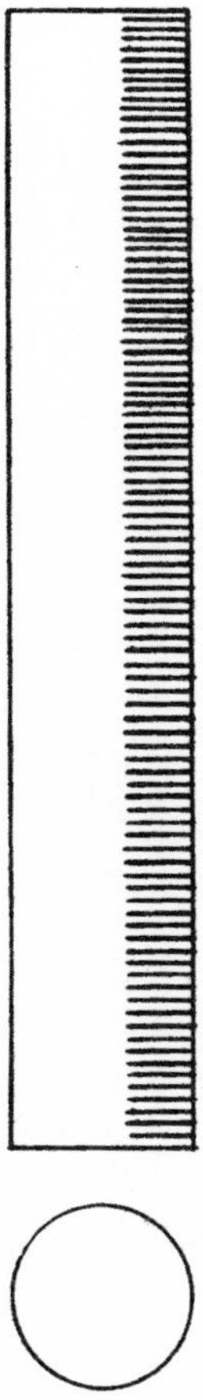

Fig. 13.

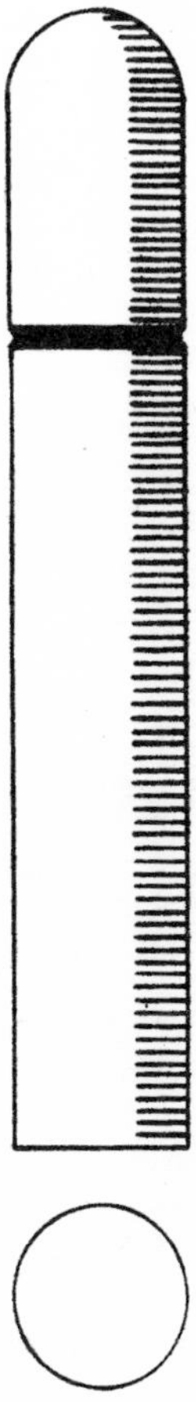

Fig. 14.

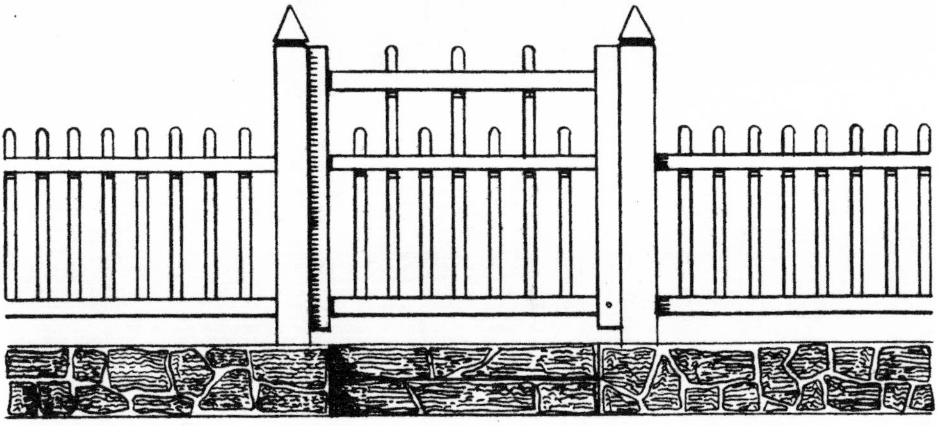

Fig. 15.

*FIG. 16.*

JOHN BROWN HOUSE
Providence, Rhode Iſland


*FIG. 17.*

GENESSEE COUNTRY VILLAGE
Mumford, New York


*FIG. 18.*

COLONIAL WILLIAMSBURG
Williamſburg, Virginia


*FIG. 19.*

GERMANTOWN
Philadelphia, Pennſylvania


*FIG. 20.*

GERMANTOWN
Philadelphia, Pennſylvania

Plate 35.

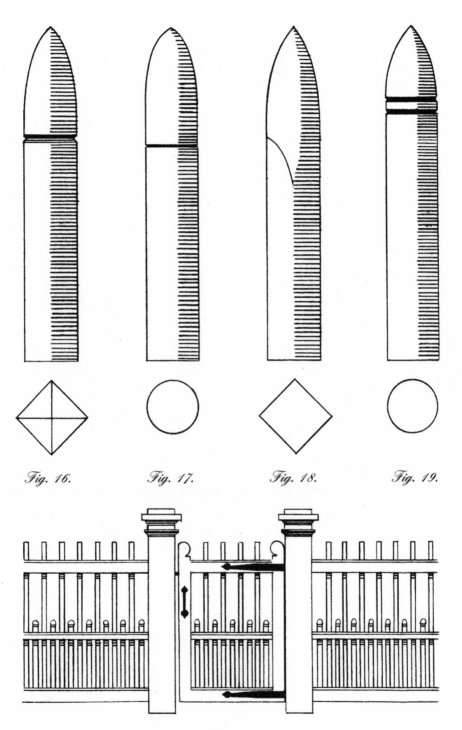

Fig. 16.          Fig. 17.          Fig. 18.          Fig. 19.

Fig. 20.

Plate 36.

# OF PANELS

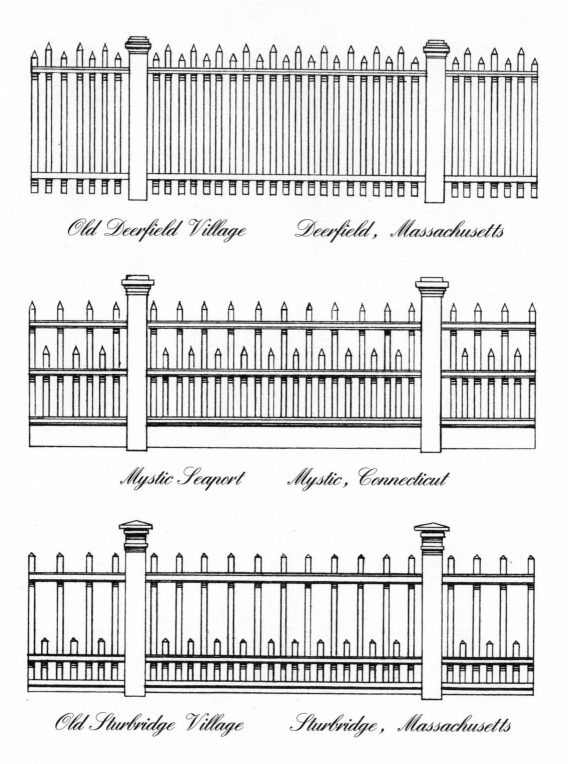

Old Deerfield Village          Deerfield, Massachusetts

Mystic Seaport          Mystic, Connecticut

Old Sturbridge Village          Sturbridge, Massachusetts

Plate 37.

# OF PANELS

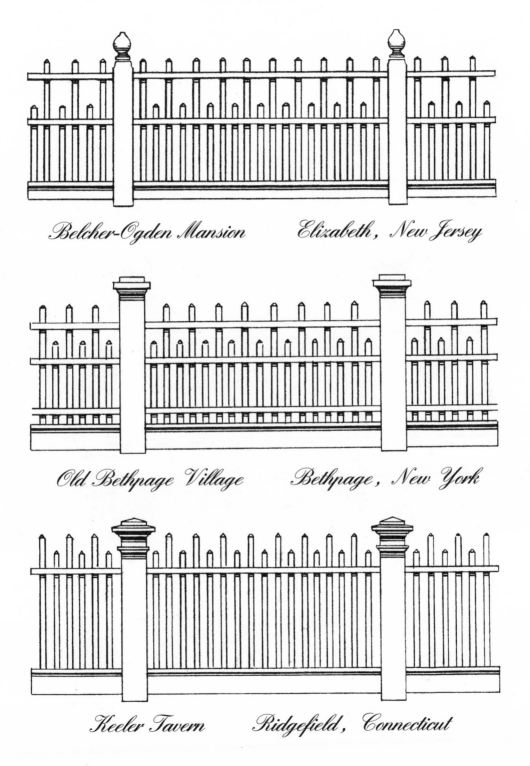

*Belcher-Ogden Mansion      Elizabeth, New Jersey*

*Old Bethpage Village      Bethpage, New York*

*Keeler Tavern      Ridgefield, Connecticut*

Plate 38.

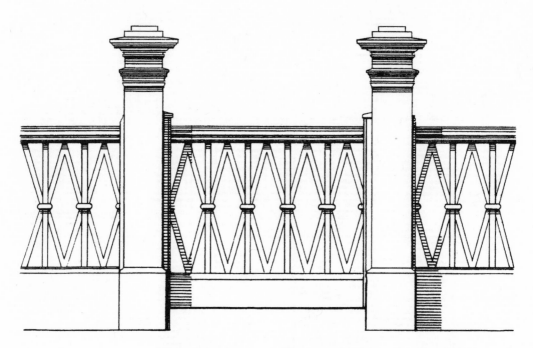

*Newburyport, Massachusetts*

*Plate 39.*

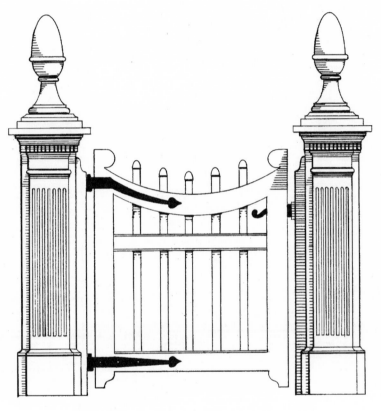

*Newburyport, Massachusetts*

Plate 40.

*Litchfield, Connecticut*

Plate 41.

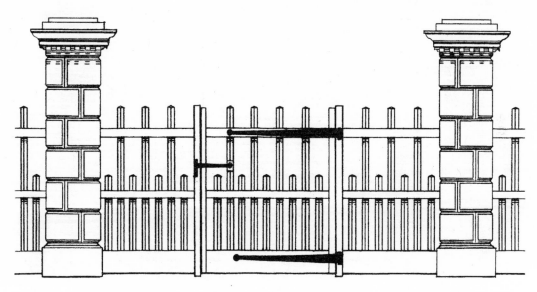

The Hatheway House     Suffield, Connecticut

*Plate 42.*

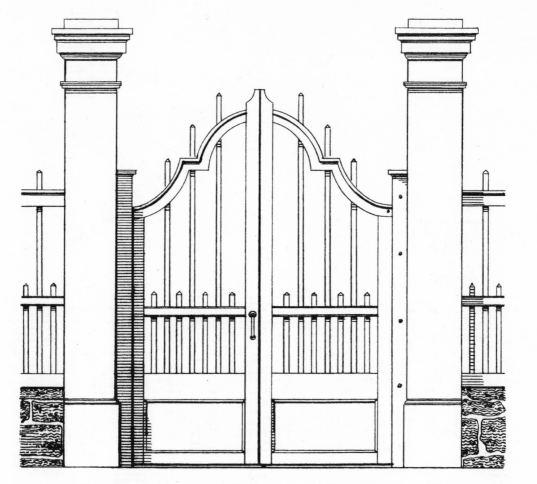

*Governor Stephen Hopkins House*      *Providence, Rhode Island*

Plate 43.

John Paul Jones House       Portsmouth, New Hampshire

Plate 44.

Lady Pepperrell House          Kittery Point,   Maine

# CHAP. V.

*Of* FENCES IN THE CHINESE TASTE

*FIG. 1.*

# COLONIAL WILLIAMSBURG
Williamſburg, Virginia


*FIG. 2.*

# COLONIAL WILLIAMSBURG
Williamſburg, Virginia


*FIG. 3.*

Litchfield, Connecticut


*FIG. 4.*

Duxbury, Maſſachuſetts


*FIG. 5.*

# OLD STURBRIDGE VILLAGE
Sturbridge, Maſſachuſetts

Plate 45.

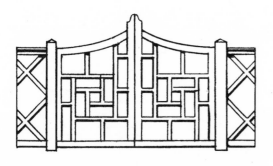

Fig. 1.

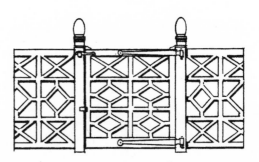

Fig. 2.

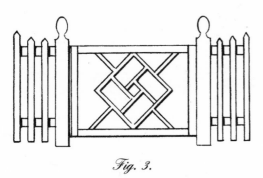

Fig. 3.

Fig. 4.

Fig. 5.

*Plate 46.*

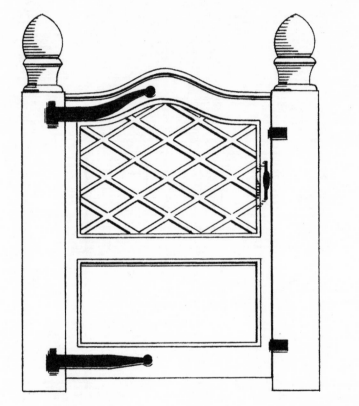

*Burgwin-Wright House*      *Wilmington, North Carolina*

*Plate 47.*

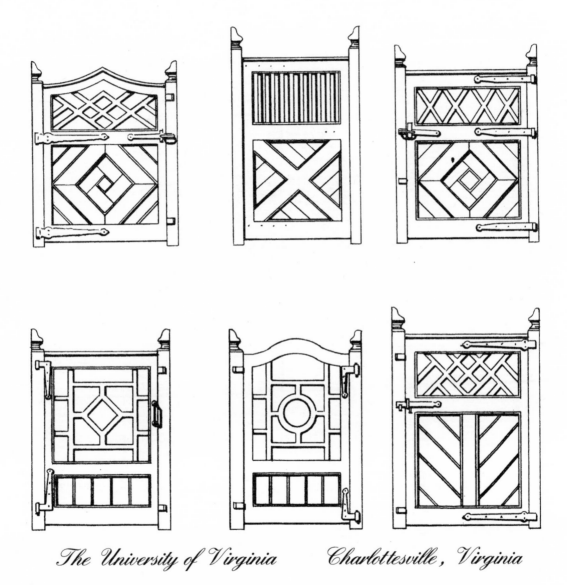

*The University of Virginia     Charlottesville, Virginia*

Plate 48.

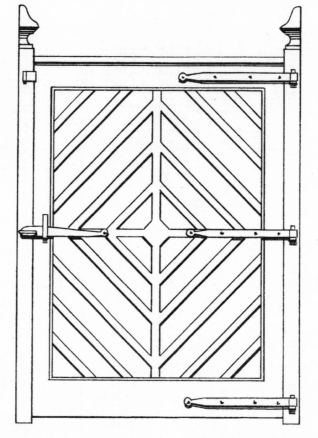

The University of Virginia        Charlottesville, Virginia

*Plate 49.*

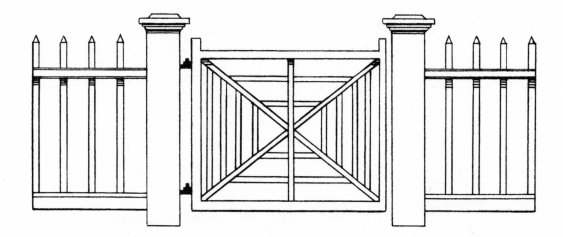

*Old York Historical Society    York , Maine*

*Plate 50.*

*Farmington, Connecticut*

*Plate 51.*

*Staunton, Virginia*

Plate 52.

Dillaway-Thomas House          Roxbury, Massachusetts

# CHAP. VI.

## *Of* BOARD FENCES

*FIG. 1.*

## OLD SALEM
Winſton-Salem, North Carolina

*FIG. 2.*

## STRAWBERY BANKE
Portſmouth, New Hampſhire

*FIG. 3.*

## OLD STURBRIDGE VILLAGE
Sturbridge, Maſſachuſetts

Plate 53.

Fig. 1.

Fig. 2.

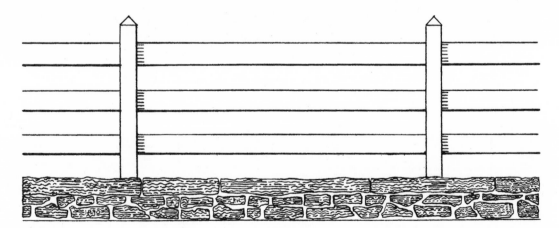

Fig. 3.

*FIG. 4.*

SOMERSET PLACE

Crefwell, North Carolina

*FIG. 5.*

COLONIAL WILLIAMSBURG

Williamfburg, Virginia

*FIG. 6.*

OLD SALEM

Winfton-Salem, North Carolina

*Plate 54.*

*Fig. 4.*

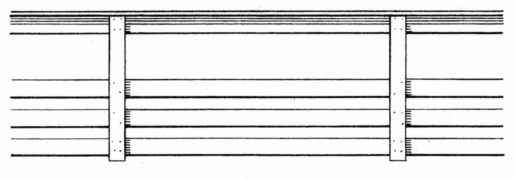

*Fig. 5.*

*Fig. 6.*

*FIG. 7.*

GENESSEE COUNTRY VILLAGE
Mumford, New York

*FIG. 8.*

COLONIAL WILLIAMSBURG
Williamſburg, Virginia

*FIG. 9.*

COLONIAL WILLIAMSBURG
Williamſburg, Virginia

*Plate 55.*

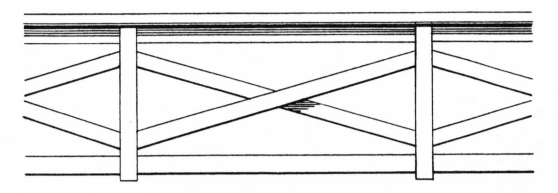

*Fig. 7.*

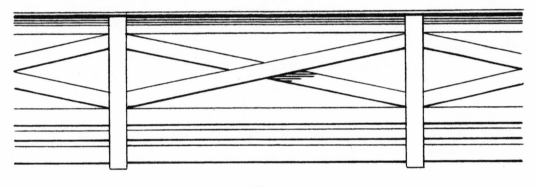

*Fig. 8.*

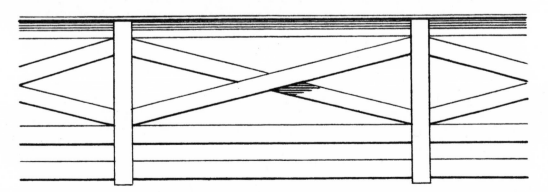

*Fig. 9.*

*FIG. 10.*

OLD STURBRIDGE VILLAGE
Sturbridge, Maffachufetts

*FIG. 11.*

COLONIAL WILLIAMSBURG
Williamfburg, Virginia

*FIG. 12.*

COLONIAL WILLIAMSBURG
Williamfburg, Virginia

Plate 56.

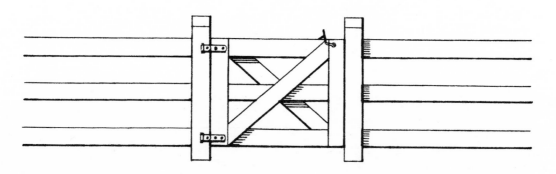

Fig. 10.

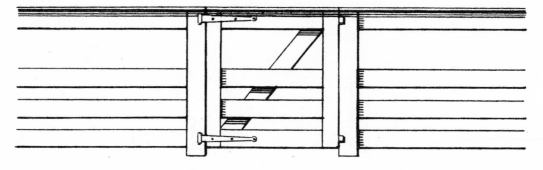

Fig. 11.

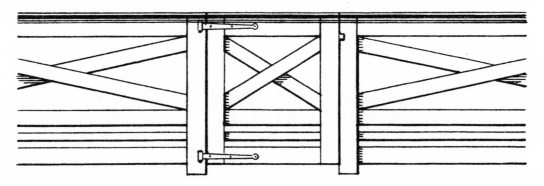

Fig. 12.

*Plate 57.*

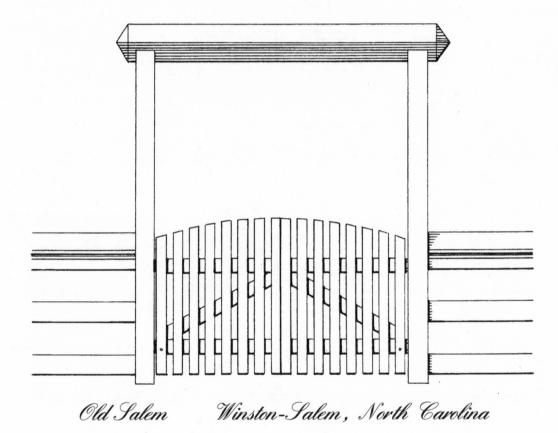

*Old Salem          Winston-Salem, North Carolina*

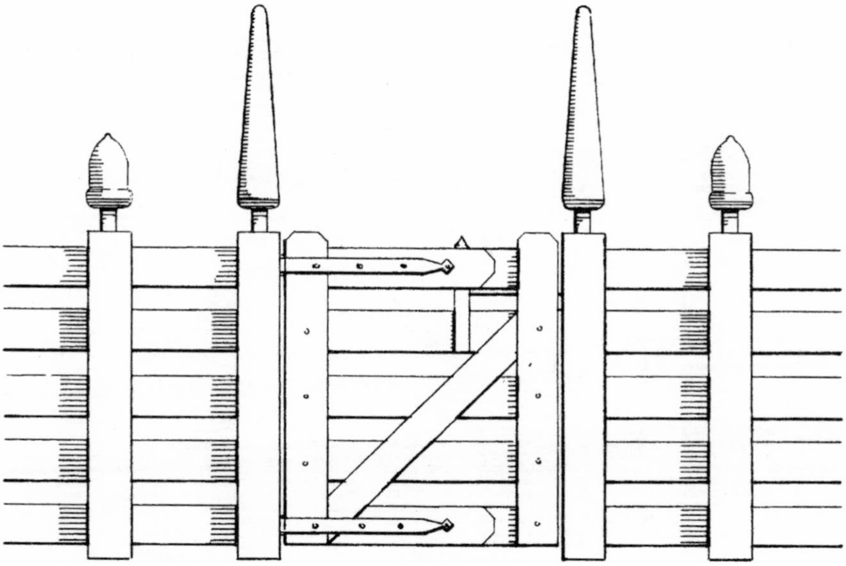

Plate 58.

*Belle Grove      Middletown, Virginia*

*Plate 59.*

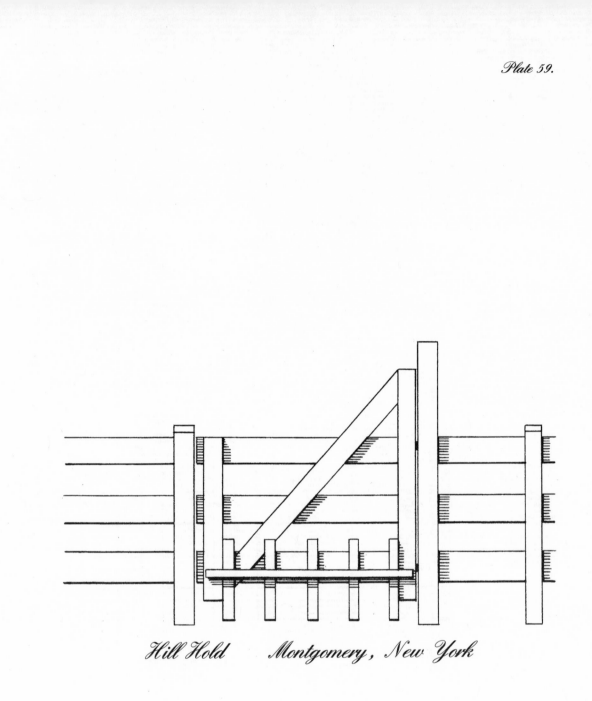

*Hill Hold        Montgomery, New York*

# CHAP. VII.

## *Of* PIERS

*FIG. 1.*
Greenfield Hill, Connecticut

*FIG. 2.*
Litchfield, Connecticut

*FIG. 3.*
Greenfield Hill, Connecticut

*FIG. 4.*
THE CAPTAIN ELISHA PHELPS HOUSE
Simſbury, Connecticut

Plate 60.

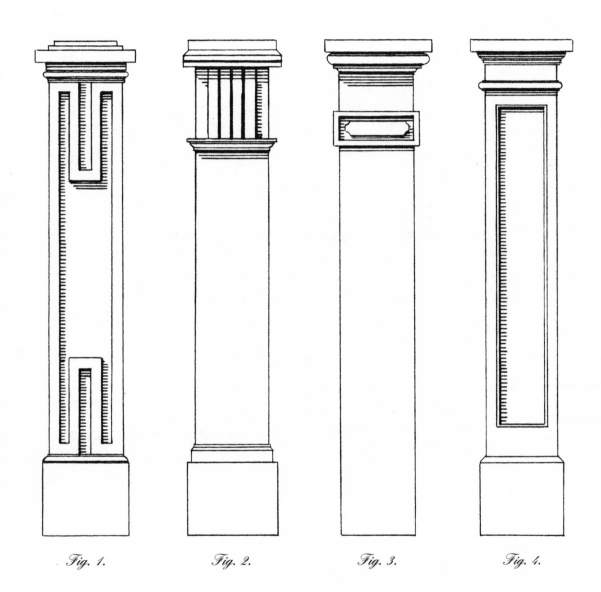

Fig. 1.          Fig. 2.          Fig. 3.          Fig. 4.

*FIG. 5.*

Effex, Connecticut


*FIG. 6.*

# OLD BETHPAGE VILLAGE

Bethpage, New York


*FIG. 7.*

# THE ISSAC ROYALL HOUSE

Medford, Maffachufetts


*FIG. 8.*

Cambridge, Maffachufetts

Plate 61.

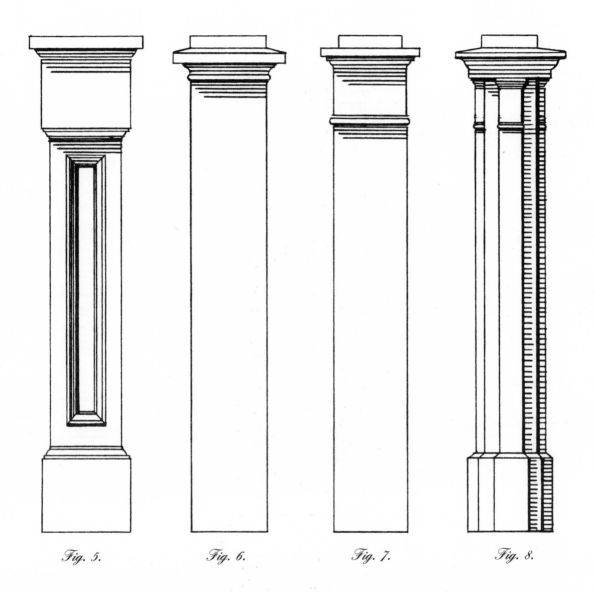

Fig. 5.        Fig. 6.        Fig. 7.        Fig. 8.

Plate 62.

*Portsmouth, New Hampshire*

Plate 63.

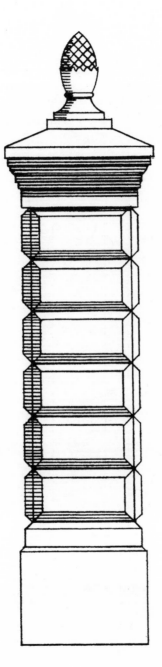

The Redwood Library        Newport, Rhode Island

Plate 64.

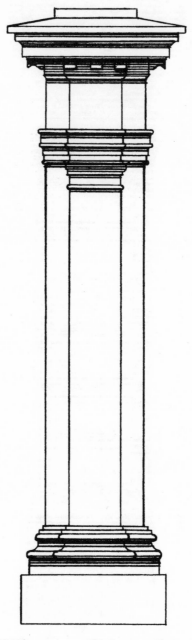

*Warren, Rhode Island*

# CHAP. VIII.

## *Of* FINIALS *for* POSTS & PIERS

*FIG. 1.*

## THE MILLER HOUSE
Hagerſtown, Maryland


*FIG. 2.*

## Frederickſburg, Virginia


*FIG. 3.*

## COLONIAL WILLIAMSBURG
Williamſburg, Virginia


*FIG. 4.*

## THE JOHN DICKINSON MANSION
Dover, Delaware

Plate 65.

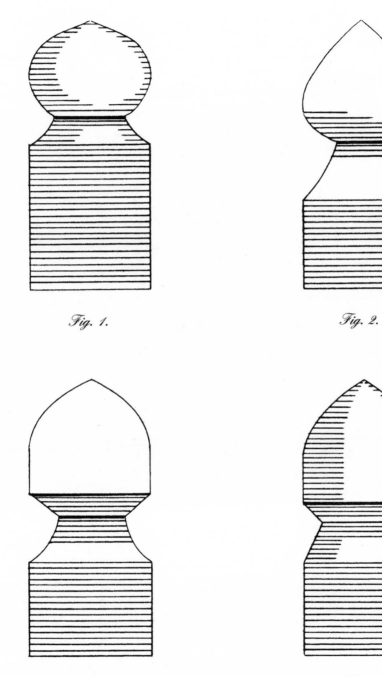

Fig. 1.

Fig. 2.

Fig. 3.

Fig. 4.

*FIG. 5.*
## OLD SALEM
Winſton Salem, North Carolina


*FIG. 6.*
## HOPE PLANTATION
Windſor, North Carolina


*FIG. 7.*
## MOUNT VERNON
Mount Vernon, Virginia


*FIG. 8.*
## STRATFORD HALL
Stratford, Virginia


*FIG. 9.*
## COLONIAL WILLIAMSBURG
Williamſburg, Virginia

*Plate 66.*

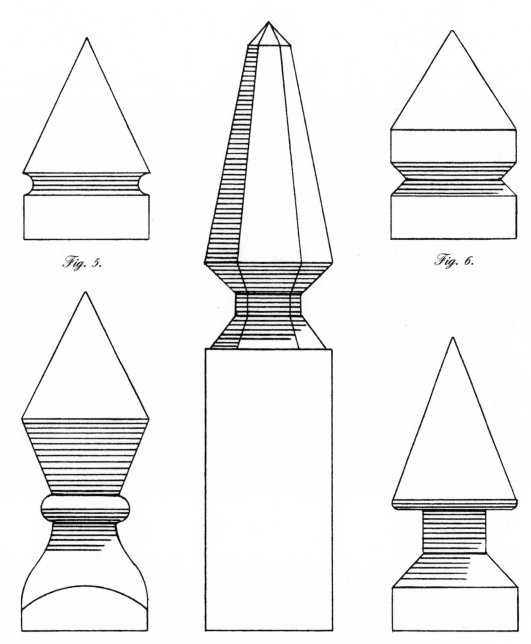

*Fig. 5.*

*Fig. 6.*

*Fig. 7.*

*Fig. 8.*

*Fig. 9.*

*Plate 67.*

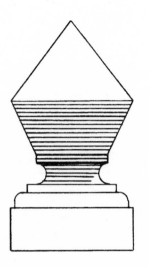

*Fig. 10.*

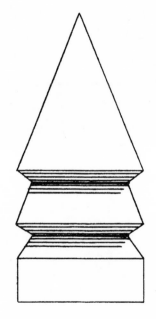

*Fig. 11.*

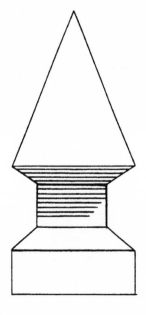

*Fig. 12.*

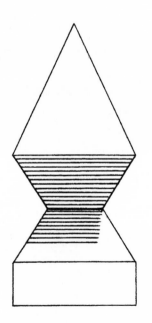

*Fig. 13.*

*Fig. 14.*

*Fig. 15.*

*FIG. 16.*

Claremont, Virginia


*FIG. 17.*

SMITH'S FORT PLANTATION

Surry, Virginia


*FIG. 18.*

COLONIAL WILLIAMSBURG

Williamſburg, Virginia

Plate 68.

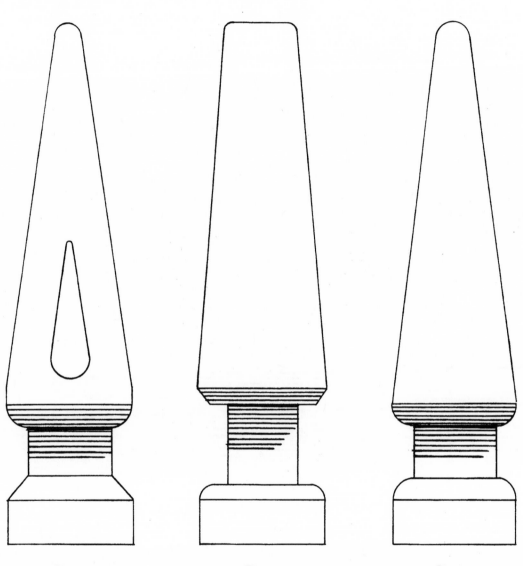

Fig. 16.          Fig. 17.          Fig. 18.

*Plate 69.*

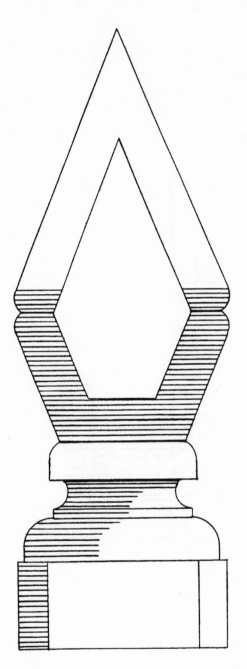

*Colonial Williamsburg     Williamsburg, Virginia*

*Plate 70.*

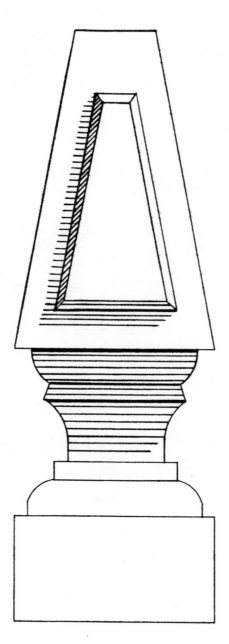

*Colonial Williamsburg*          *Williamsburg, Virginia*

*Plate 71.*

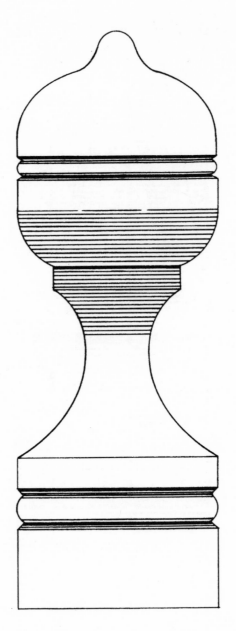

*Stratford Hall Plantation*     *Stratford, Virginia*

*Plate 72.*

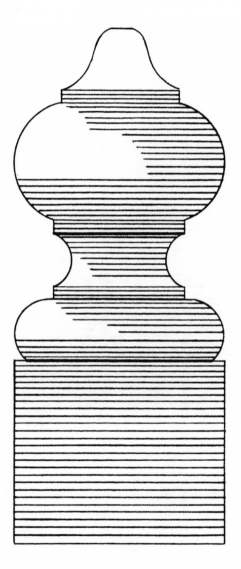

*Colonial Williamsburg*    *Williamsburg, Virginia*

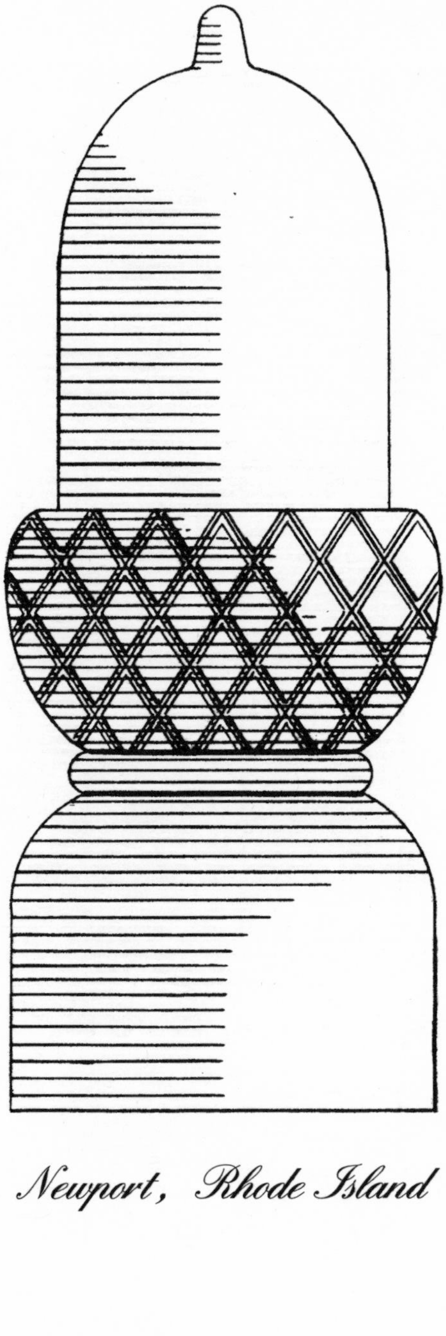

*Plate 73.*

*Newport, Rhode Island*

*Plate 74.*

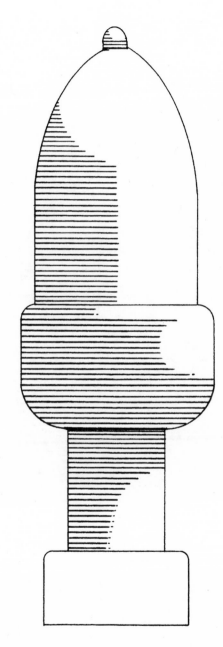

*Belle Grove        Middletown, Virginia*

*Plate 75.*

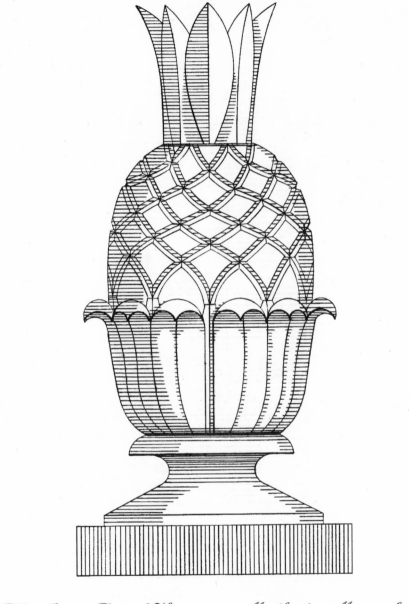

*The Isaac Royal House*     *Medford,  Massachusetts*

*Plate 76.*

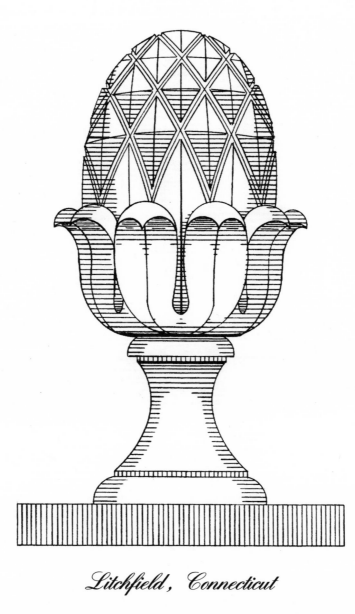

*Litchfield, Connecticut*

*Plate 77.*

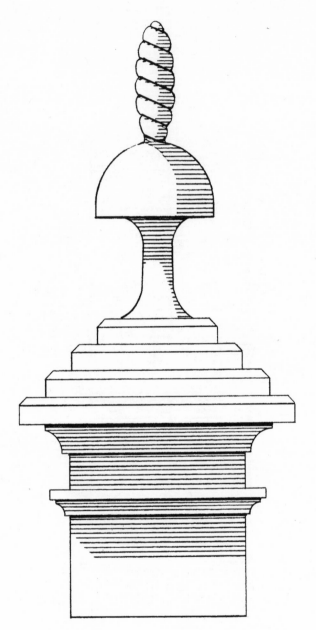

*Old Deerfield Village      Deerfield, Massachusetts*

# CHAP. IX.

*Of* CAPS *for* POSTS & PIERS

*FIG. 1.*

GENESSEE COUNTRY VILLAGE
Mumford, New York

*FIG. 2.*

GENESSEE COUNTRY VILLAGE
Mumford, New York

*FIG. 3.*

Litchfield, Connecticut

*FIG. 4.*

Princeton, New Jersey

*Plate 78.*

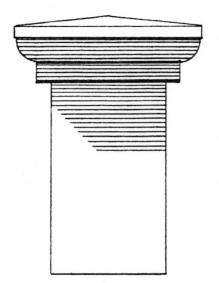

*Fig. 1.*

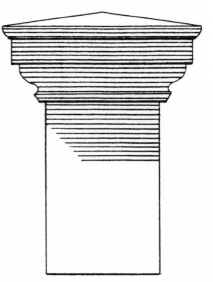

*Fig. 2.*

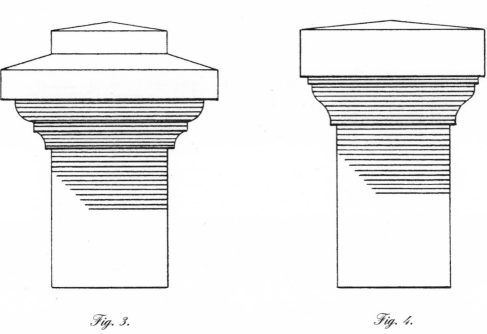

*Fig. 3.*

*Fig. 4.*

*FIG. 5.*
Newport, Rhode Ifland


*FIG. 6.*
Providence, Rhode Ifland


*FIG. 7.*
OLD STURBRIDGE VILLAGE
Sturbridge, Maffachufetts


*FIG. 8.*
THE KING CAESAR HOUSE
Duxbury, Maffachufetts

Plate 79.

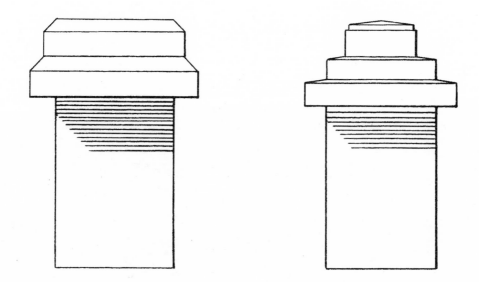

Fig. 5.

Fig. 6.

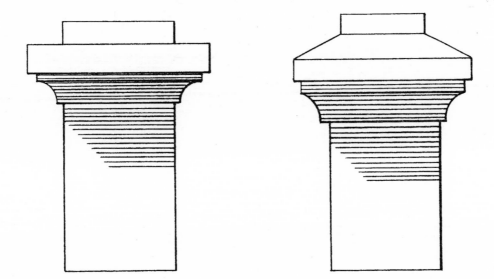

Fig. 7.

Fig. 8.

Plate 80.

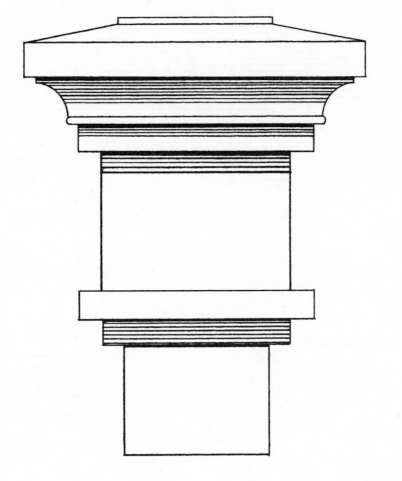

Genessee Country Village     Mumford, New York

*Plate 81.*

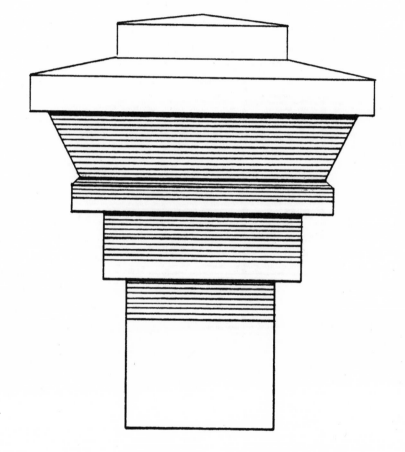

*Genessee Country Village     Mumford, New York*

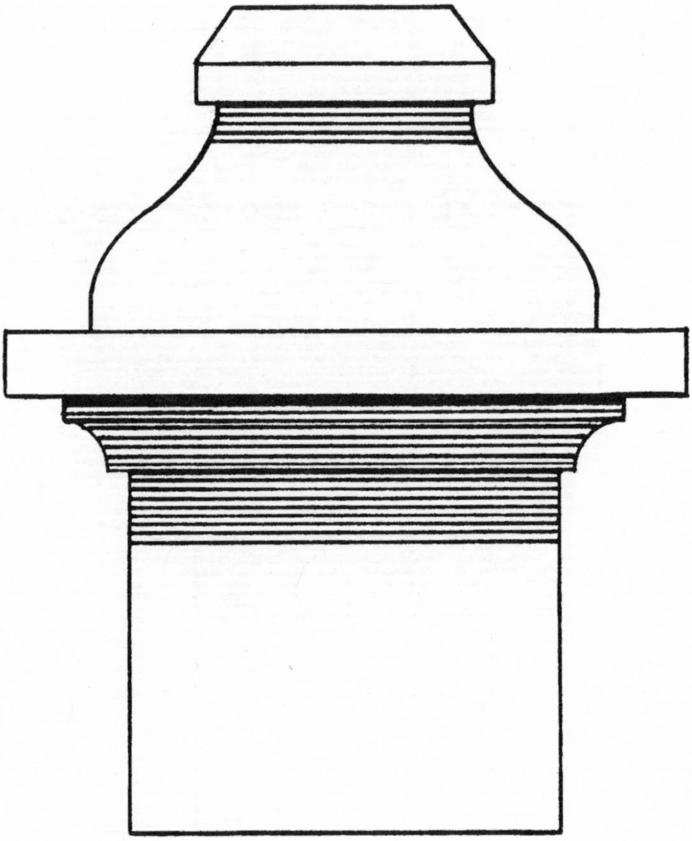

*Plate 82.*

*Old Deerfield Village*      *Deerfield, Massachusetts*

# CHAP. X.

## *Of* Urns *for* Posts & Piers

*FIG. 1.*

Newburyport, Maſſachuſetts


*FIG. 2.*

Portsmouth, New Hampſhire


*FIG. 3.*

THE LONGFELLOW HOUSE

Cambridge, Maſſachuſetts


*FIG. 4.*

Newburyport, Maſſachuſetts


*FIG. 5.*

Newburyport, Maſſachuſetts


*FIG. 6.*

Portsmouth, New Hampſhire

Plate 83.

Fig. 1.

Fig. 2.

Fig. 3.

Fig. 4.

Fig. 5.

Fig. 6.

Plate 84.

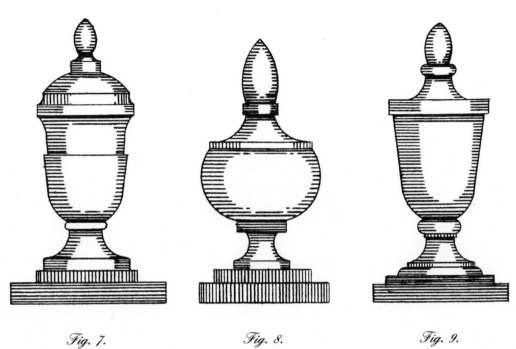

Fig. 7.

Fig. 8.

Fig. 9.

Fig. 10.

Fig. 11.

Fig. 12.

*Plate 85.*

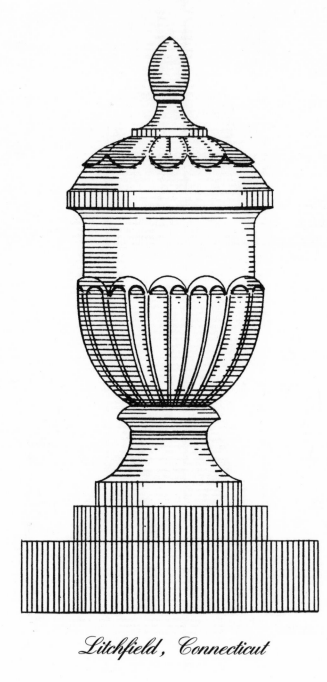

*Litchfield, Connecticut*

*Plate 86.*

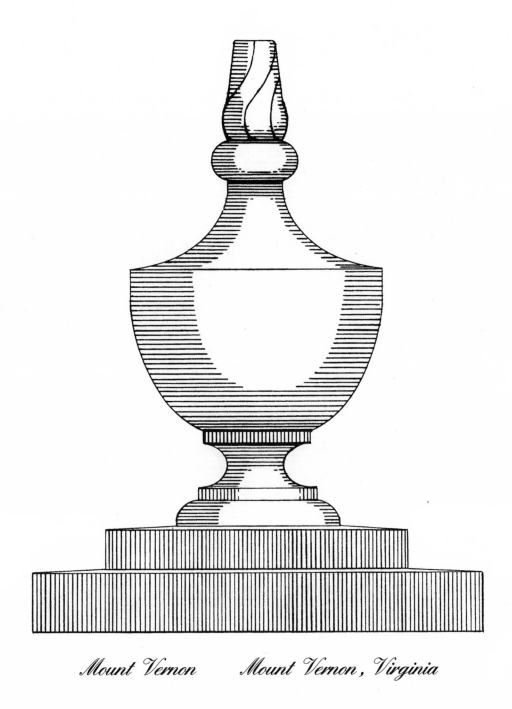

*Mount Vernon        Mount Vernon, Virginia*

*Plate 87.*

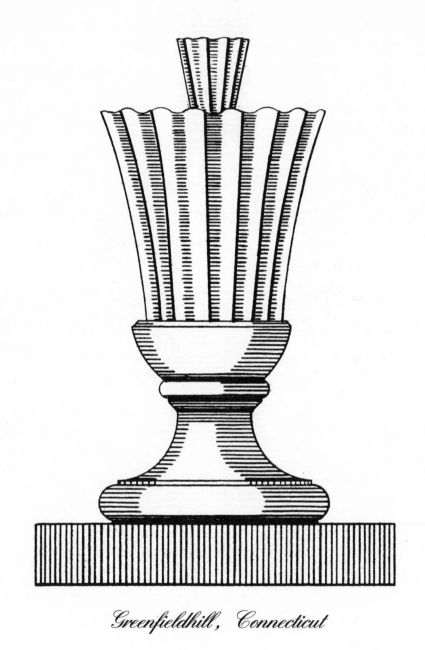

*Greenfieldhill, Connecticut*

*Plate 88.*

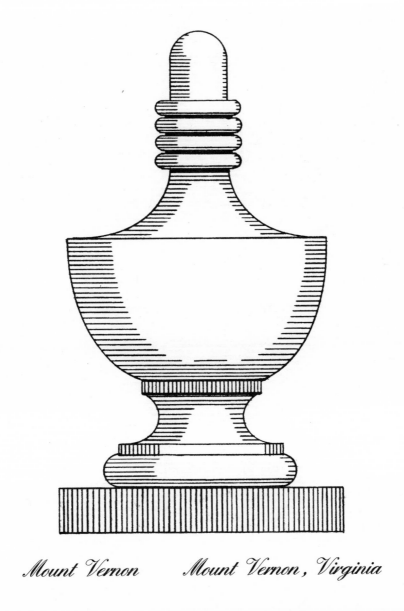

*Mount Vernon*      *Mount Vernon, Virginia*

*Plate 89.*

*The Sewall House     Bath, Maine*

# CHAP. XI.

*Of* BALLS *for* PIERS, PARAPETS

& GARDEN WALLS

*FIG. 1.*

OLD STURBRIDGE VILLAGE
Sturbridge, Maffachufetts


*FIG. 2.*

THE LONGFELLOW HOUSE
Cambridge, Maffachufetts


*FIG. 3.*

THE HATHEWAY HOUSE
Suffield, Connecticut


*FIG. 4.*

Farmington, Connecticut

Plate 90.

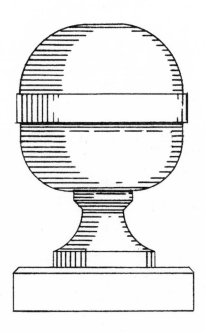

Fig. 1.

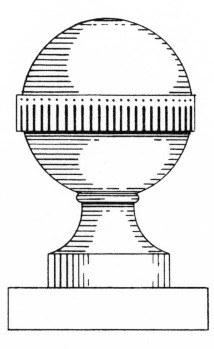

Fig. 2.

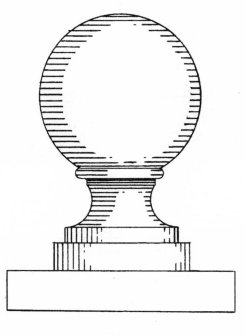

Fig. 3.

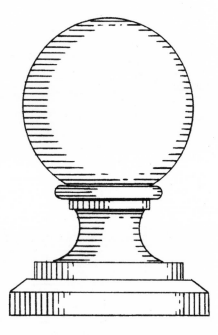

Fig. 4.

*Plate 91.*

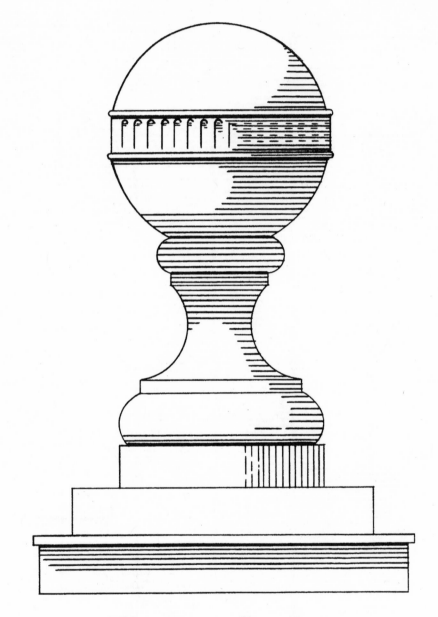

*Cambridge, Massachusetts*

*Plate 92.*

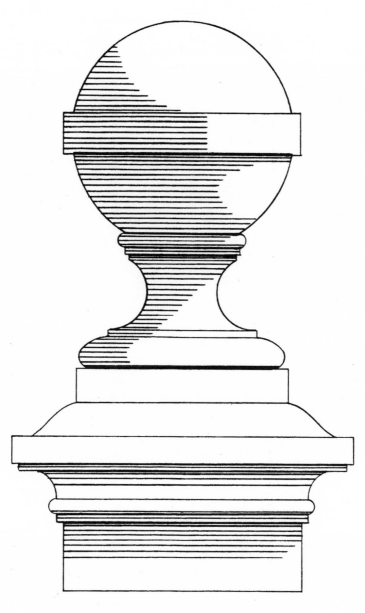

*Rensselaerville, New York*

PART II

# FENCES

OF

CAPE COD

*A COLLECTION MOST COMPLETE*

OF

## FENCES

FROM CAPE COD AND THE ENVIRONS.

FOR

COUNTRY MANSIONS, SUBURBAN VILLAS, and COTTAGES.

INCLUDING IN GREAT DETAIL

BALLS, CAPS, FINIALS, AND URNS

PLATE 93.

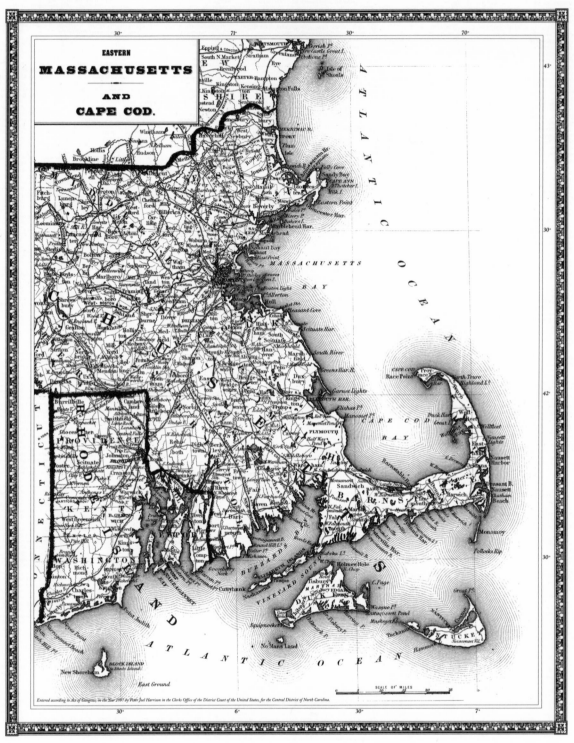

EASTERN
# MASSACHUSETTS
## AND
## CAPE COD.

WHEN I was but a young lad my father and mother brought my two brothers and me to Cape Cod. It was a return to home as it were, since my family came to these beaches in 1688. It was a delightful time with my family that summer. My brothers and I frolicked in the waves, collected beach plums, and gathered pails brimming full of sea shells. In the late afternoon, we would make our way back passing cottages drenched with sun. Each surrounded with white fences, all tumbled over with fragrant pink roses. It is a memory sweet that strongly lingers with me these many years later.

Now I am a father; and like my father before me, I have returned to Cape Cod with my son so he too will know his beginnings. While there, I was once again taken captive by the charm of this place and it came to me that I should record some of these beauties for others to enjoy. Thus I have come to this work; FENCES of CAPE COD.

For many seasons I traveled the wide ways and narrow lanes of Provincetown, Chatham, Falmouth, and Sandwich. I ventured north to Duxbury and Boston; then west to New Bedford and Fall River. By steamship I ferried to Martha's Vineyard and Nantucket recording all I saw; always asking the good Lord to turn my head so nothing of value would go amiss.

Now quite done, I lay before you this fourth work with all hopes that it will give you much pleasure, and enable those like myself engaged in the noble art of building.

PETER JOEL HARRISON

# CHAPTER XII.

CONSTRUCTION

*In building a substantial fence whether for garden, orchard or to mark a boundary between estates, each component must be carefully considered.*

The timber for posts should be of seasoned heart wood. Red cedar makes the best posts. Then listed according to desirability; white oak, chestnut or black locust. Posts are sawn in lengths seven feet long and cut to either four or six inches square. All fence work should be planed neat. Each post should be painted with a  mixture of boiled linseed oil and pulverized charcoal. This measure will greatly aid in their longevity. Post holes should be dug three feet deep and eight feet to ten feet apart. Drive a post into each hole with a wooden maul; as in Figure 1.

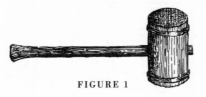

FIGURE 1

Large stones placed in each hole will keep posts firm against all kinds of stock; as illustrated in Figure 2 The earth around each post should be packed as firmly as possible. This is best done with a fine piece of oak three feet six inches long, and rounded off at one end to fit the hand.

FIGURE 2

The best lumber for stringers is white oak, poplar or pine. Cut a mortise into each post to hold stringers. Spread each mortise and tenon with thick paint before putting them in place. This measure will increase their usefulness.

Pine wood is best for boards and pickets. Its light weight will prevent the stringers from sagging over time. A horse or bench as illustrated in Figure 3. is put to good use in cutting pickets. The finished length of common pickets is three feet six inches.

FIGURE 3

Fancy work with notches as in Figure 4 is accomplished with a compass saw or foot powered scroll saw.

FIGURE 4

Using ten penny annealed steel nails, hammer each picket or board into place. Spacing should be done according to the desired purpose. A good garden fence is laid out with pickets one to two and one half inches apart. This will prevent even a small rabbit from passing through. The bottom of each picket should be approximately two inches from the ground. Where rooting is an expected annoyance a skirt or "Dog Board" is put at the foot of the pickets. When all is satisfactorily completed a good coat of crude petroleum, applied before painting, will preserve the fence and save more than its cost on paint needed.

PLATE 94.

# PANELS

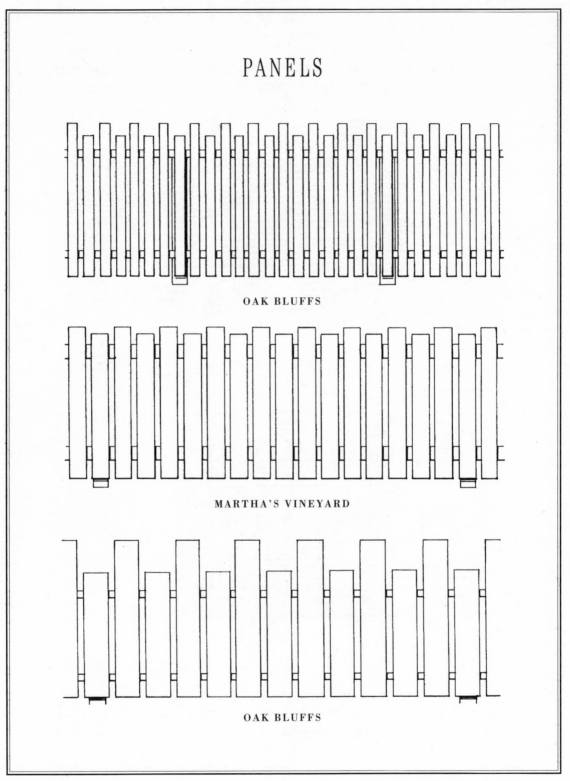

OAK BLUFFS

MARTHA'S VINEYARD

OAK BLUFFS

PLATE 95.

# PANELS

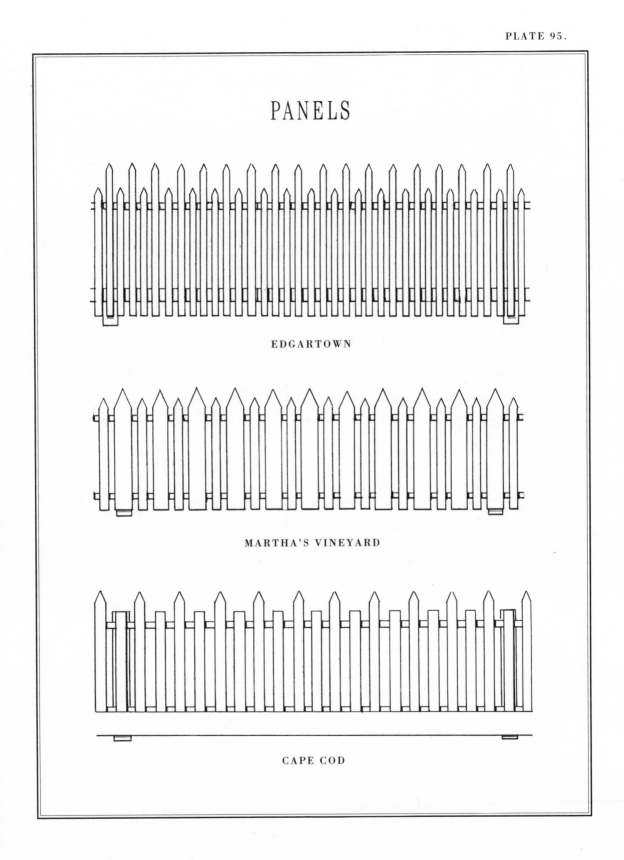

EDGARTOWN

MARTHA'S VINEYARD

CAPE COD

PLATE 96.

# PANELS

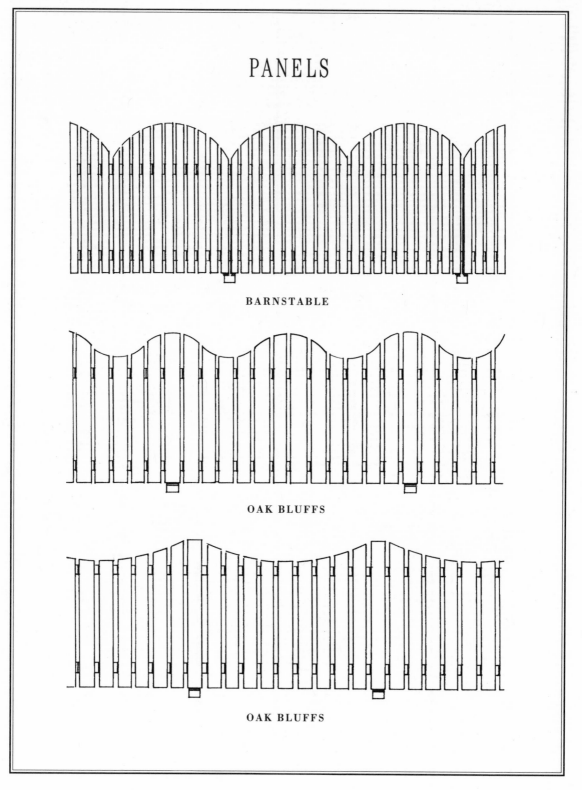

BARNSTABLE

OAK BLUFFS

OAK BLUFFS

PLATE 97.

# GATE BRACING

PROVINCETOWN

PLATE 98.

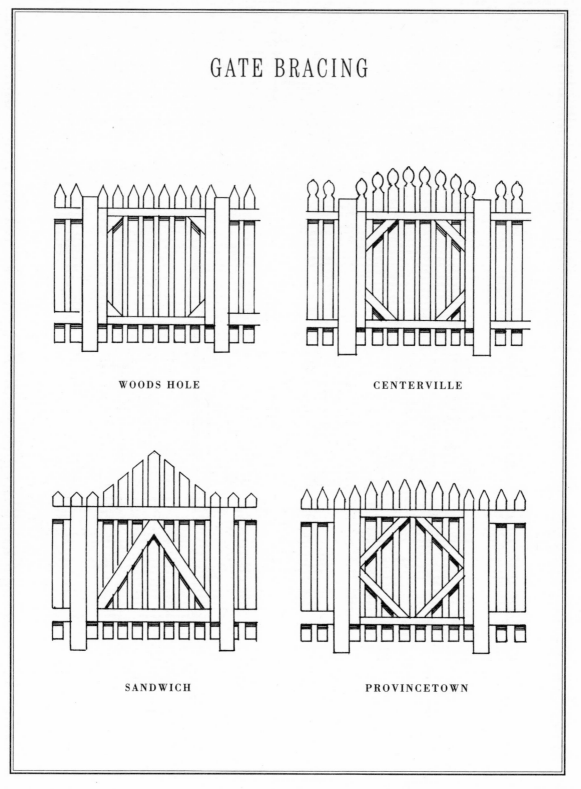

# GATE BRACING

WOODS HOLE

CENTERVILLE

SANDWICH

PROVINCETOWN

PLATE 99.

# GATE BRACING

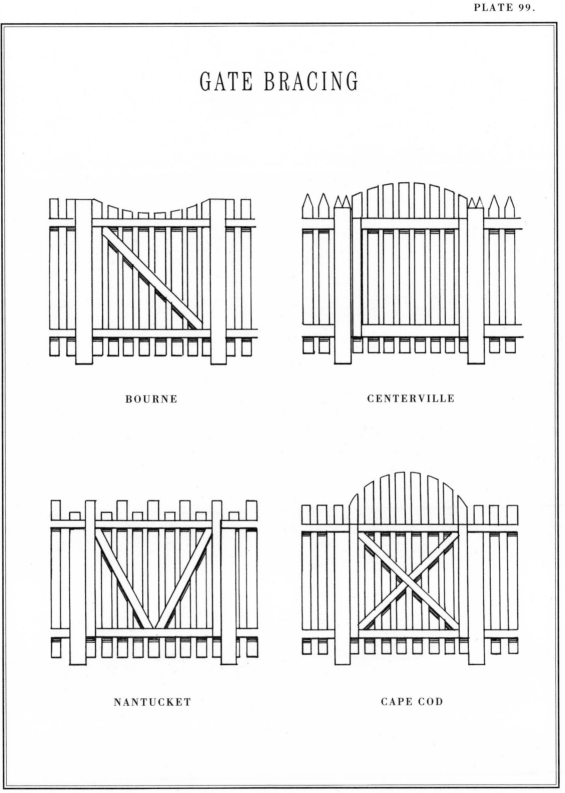

BOURNE

CENTERVILLE

NANTUCKET

CAPE COD

PLATE 100.

# STRAP HINGES

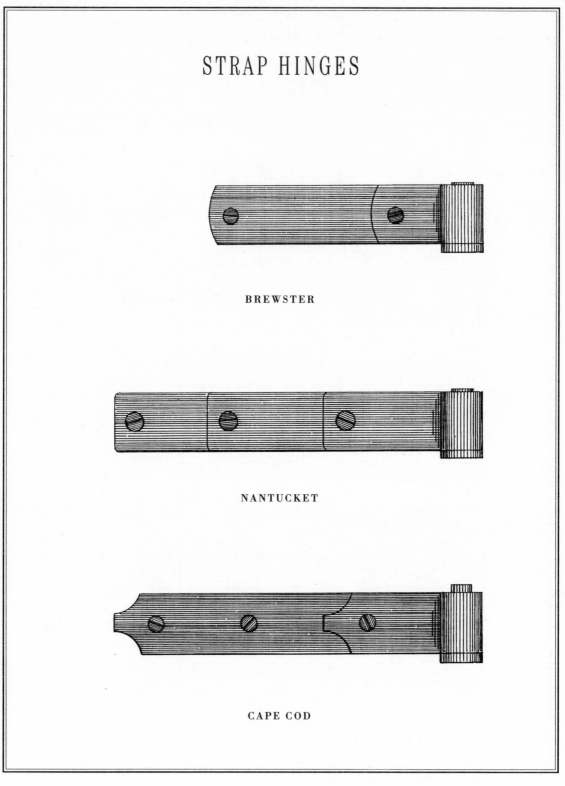

BREWSTER

NANTUCKET

CAPE COD

PLATE 101

# STRAP HINGES

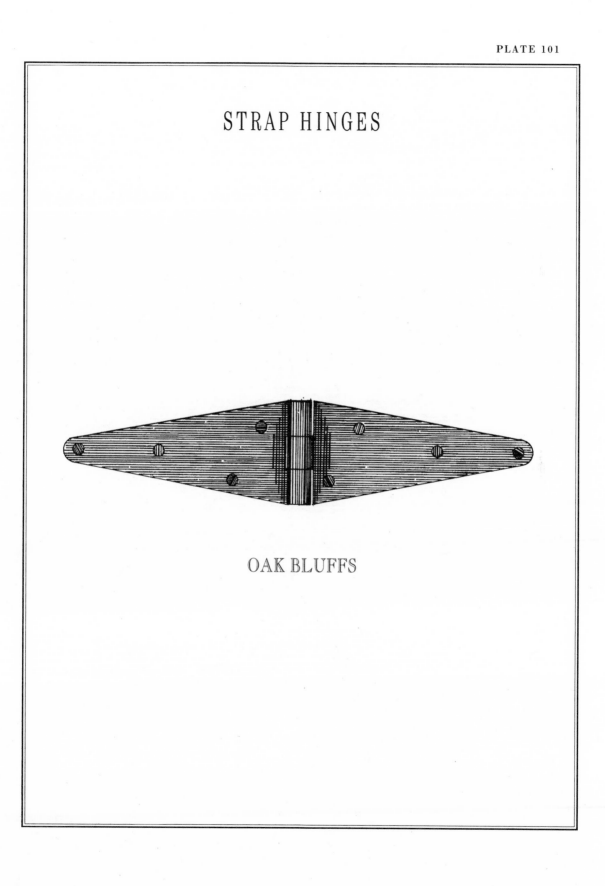

OAK BLUFFS

PLATE 102.

# STEEL GATE LATCH

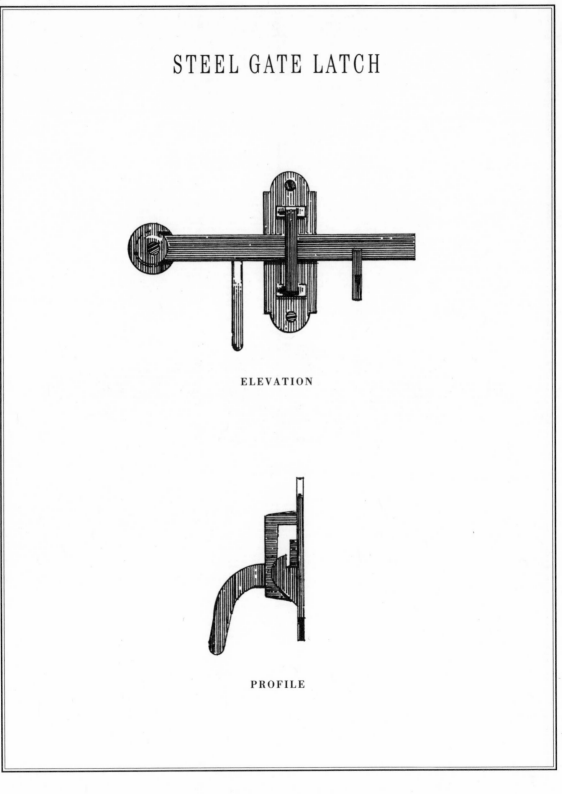

ELEVATION

PROFILE

PLATE 103.

# WOODEN GATE LATCH

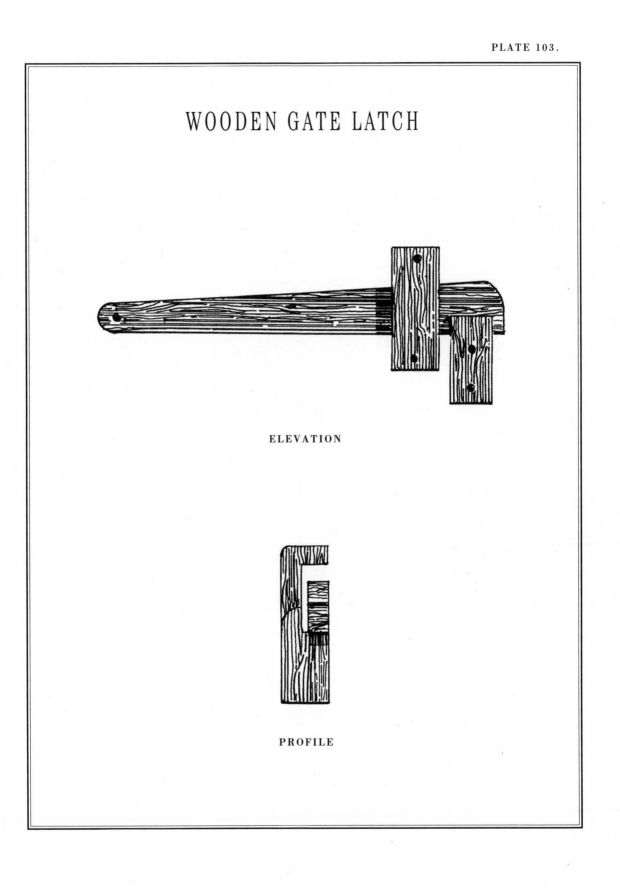

ELEVATION

PROFILE

PLATE 104.

# COMMON PICKET

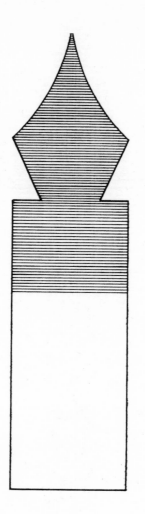

The painting of the head of a common picket is most pleasing. Particularly when it is done in harmony with the shutters or blinds of the house. The colours brown, forest green, blue, and gray are most agreeable with nature.

# CHAPTER XIII.

---

## POSTS

PLATE 105.

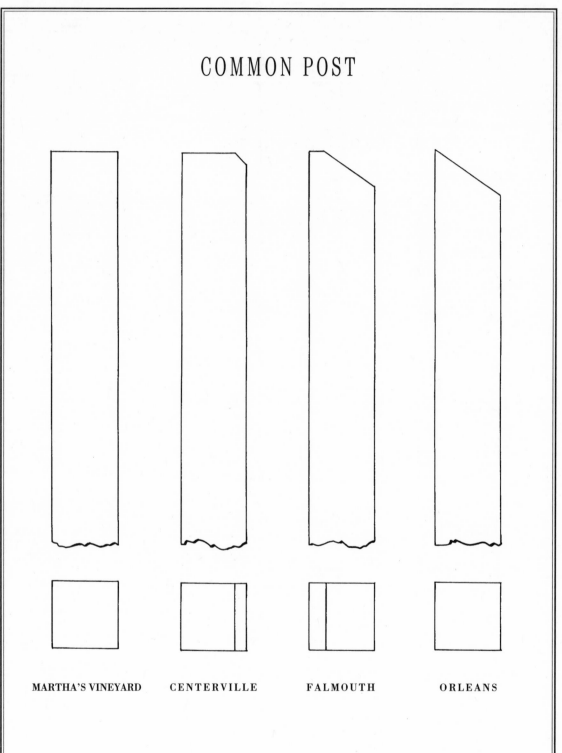

# COMMON POST

MARTHA'S VINEYARD    CENTERVILLE    FALMOUTH    ORLEANS

PLATE 106.

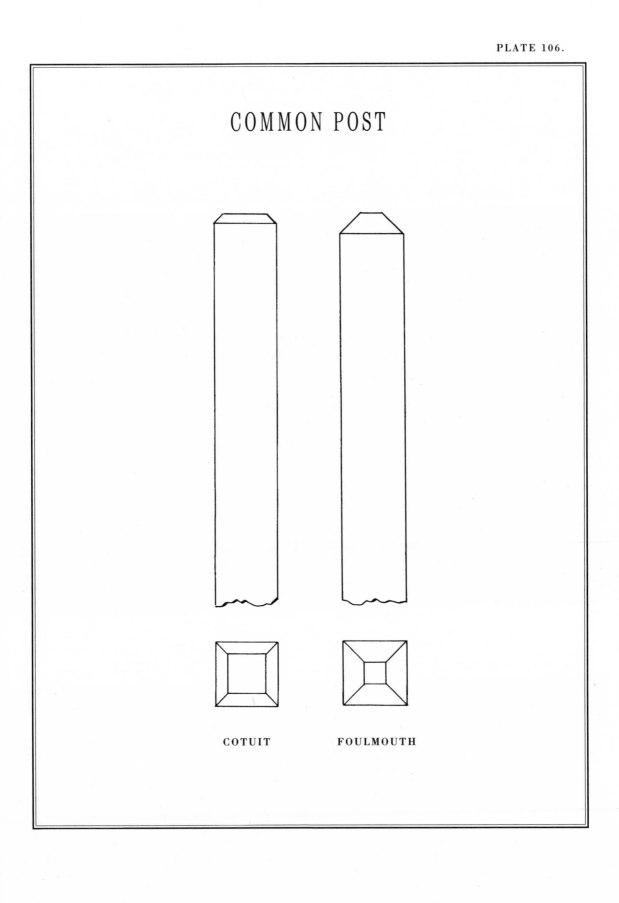

# COMMON POST

COTUIT          FOULMOUTH

PLATE 107.

# COMMON POST

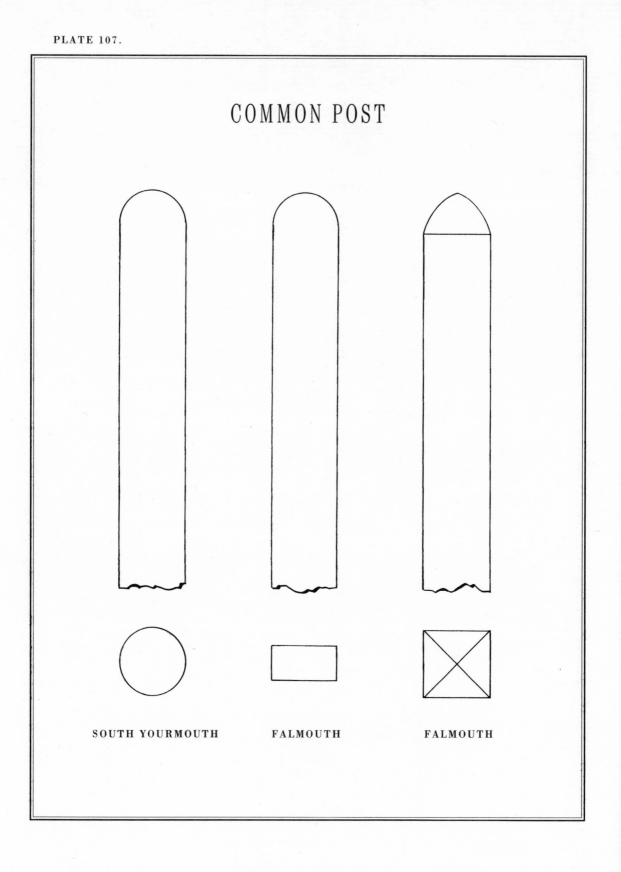

SOUTH YOURMOUTH      FALMOUTH      FALMOUTH

PLATE 108.

# TURNED POST

SOUTH CHATHAM          CHATHAM          SOUTH CHATHAM

PLATE 109.

# TURNED POST

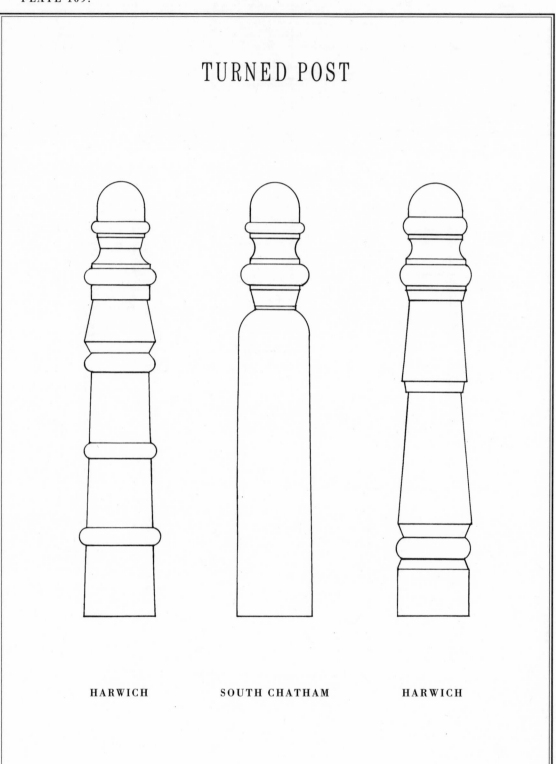

HARWICH            SOUTH CHATHAM            HARWICH

PLATE 110.

# TURNED POST

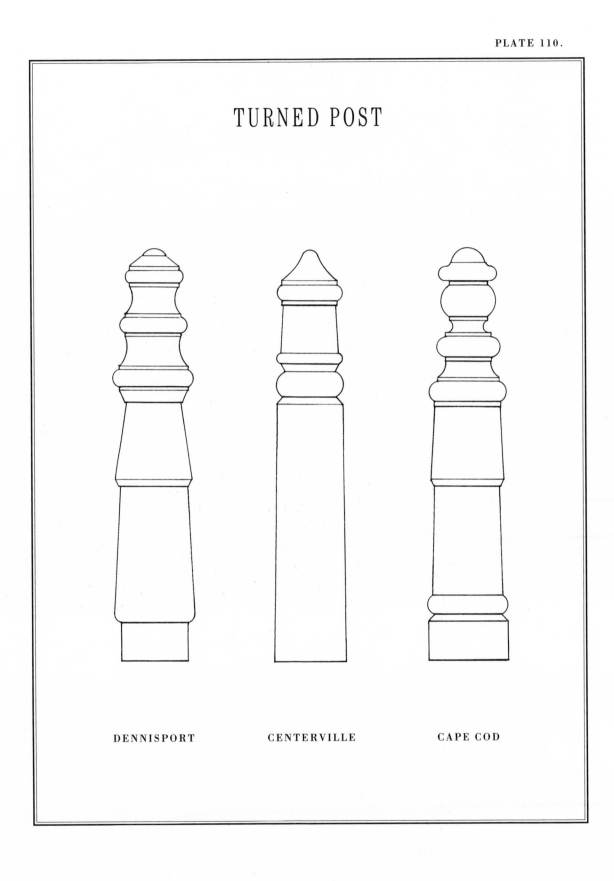

DENNISPORT          CENTERVILLE          CAPE COD

PLATE 111.

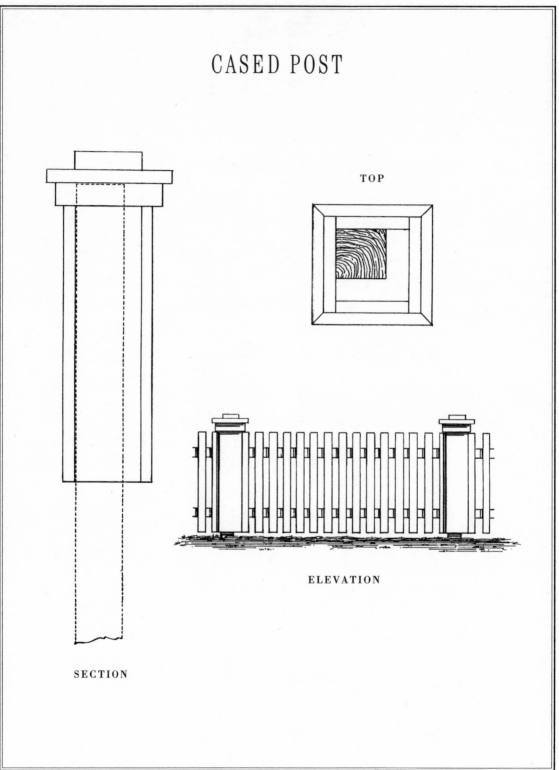

# CASED POST

TOP

ELEVATION

SECTION

# CHAPTER XIV.

---

## COMMON PICKETS

PLATE 112.

PROVINCETOWN

PLATE 113.

MARTHA'S VINEYARD          NANTUCKET          OAK BLUFFS

PLATE 114.

ORLEANS

PLATE 115.

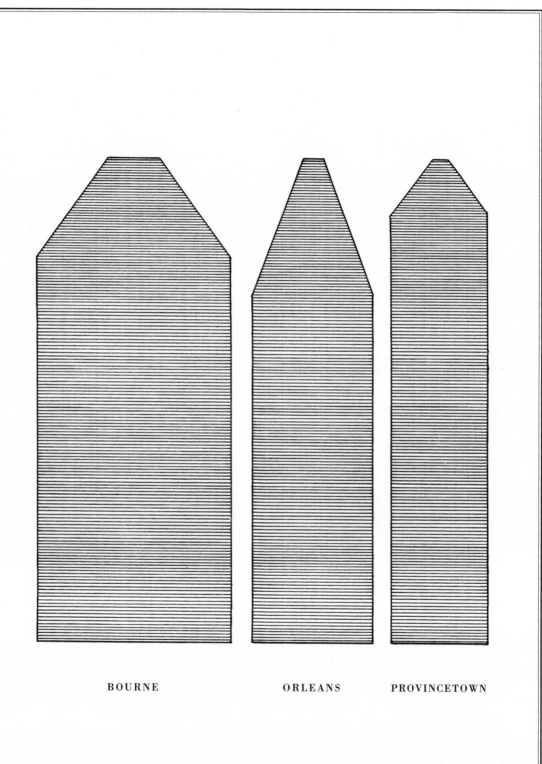

BOURNE          ORLEANS     PROVINCETOWN

PLATE 116.

COTUIT

PLATE 117.

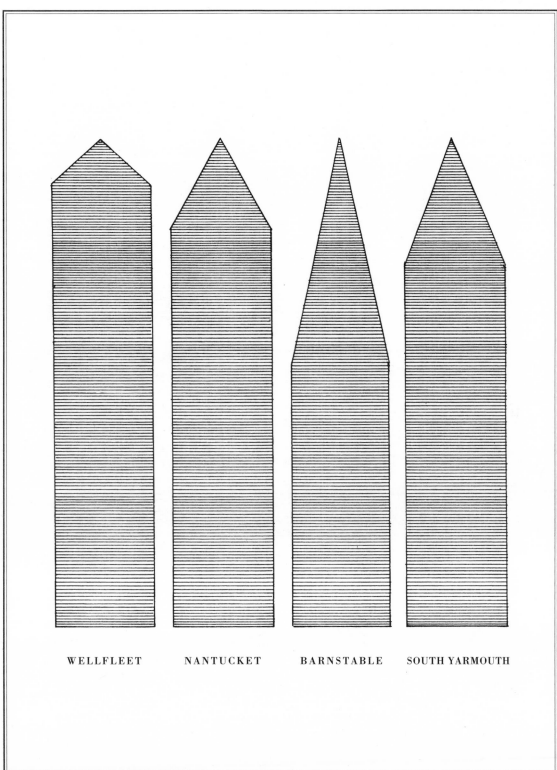

WELLFLEET          NANTUCKET          BARNSTABLE          SOUTH YARMOUTH

PLATE 118.

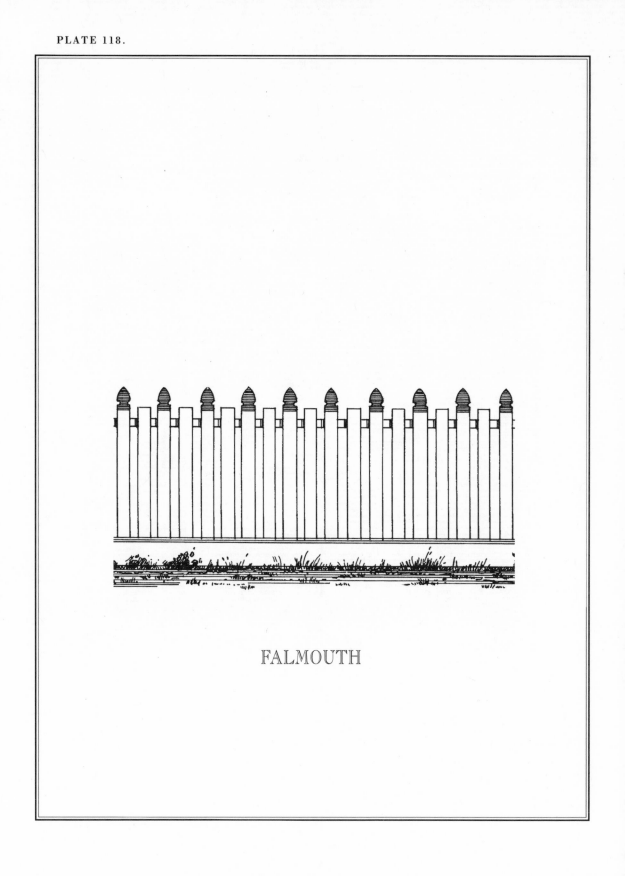

FALMOUTH

PLATE 119.

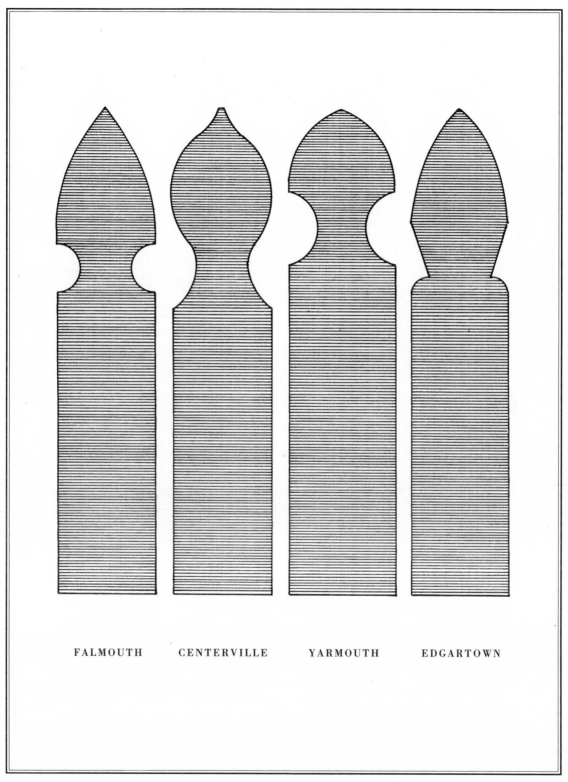

FALMOUTH     CENTERVILLE     YARMOUTH     EDGARTOWN

PLATE 120.

CAPE COD

PLATE 121.

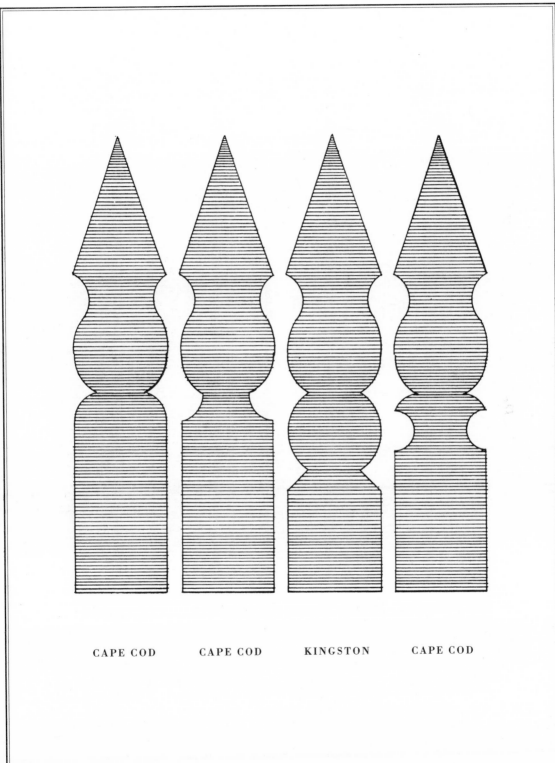

CAPE COD     CAPE COD     KINGSTON     CAPE COD

PLATE 122.

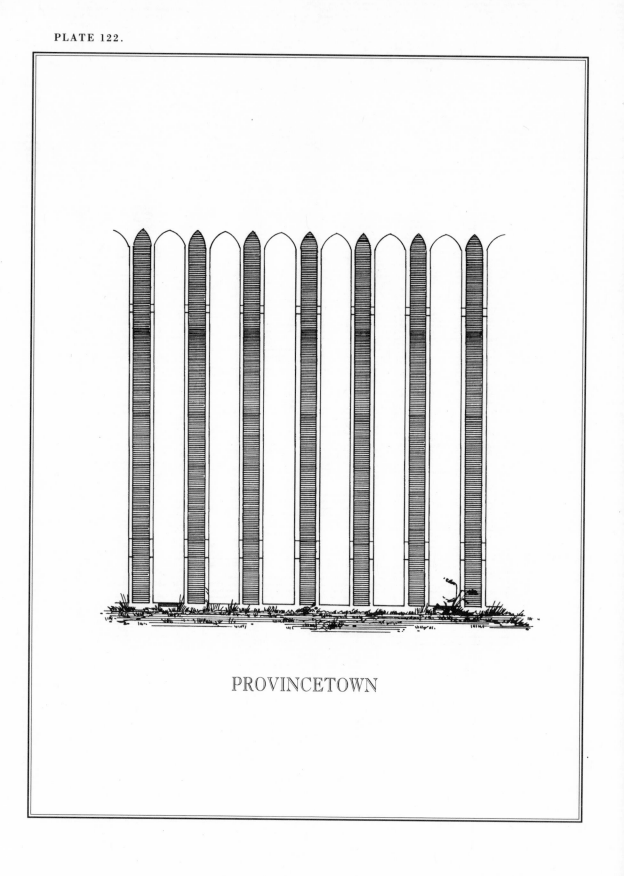

PROVINCETOWN

PLATE 123.

PROVINCETOWN                    PROVINCETOWN

PLATE 124.

NANTUCKET

# CHAPTER XV.

---

## COMMON PICKETS WITH CAP RAIL

PLATE 125.

# CAP RAILS

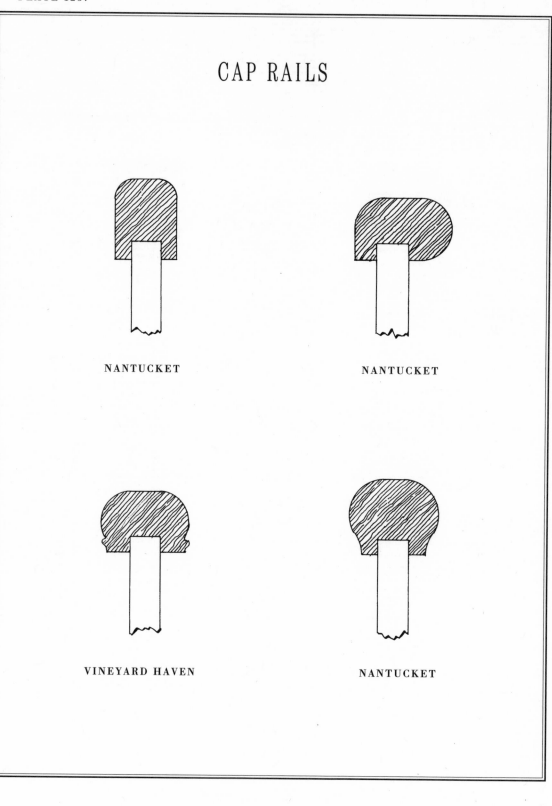

NANTUCKET

NANTUCKET

VINEYARD HAVEN

NANTUCKET

PLATE 126.

# CAP RAILS

NANTUCKET

PROVINCETOWN

NANTUCKET

NANTUCKET

PLATE 127.

CHATHAM

PLATE 128.

NANTUCKET

PLATE 129.

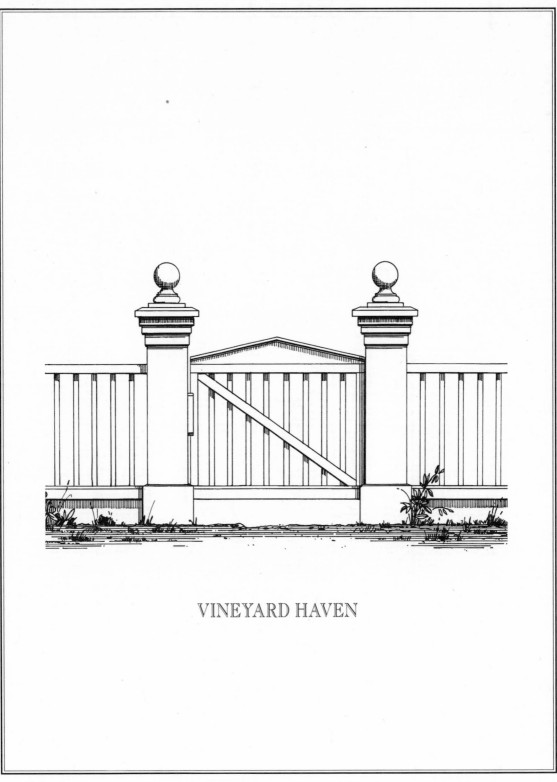

VINEYARD HAVEN

PLATE 130.

EDGARTOWN

PLATE 131.

VINEYARD HAVEN

# CHAPTER XVI.

————

## ORNAMENTAL AND FANCY FENCES

PLATE 132.

BREWSTER

PLATE 133.

WELLFLEET

PLATE 134.

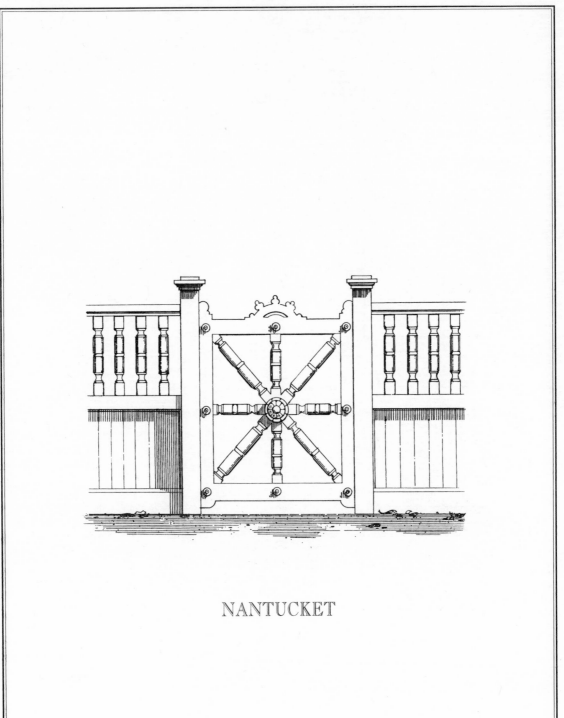

NANTUCKET

PLATE 135.

NANTUCKET

PLATE 136.

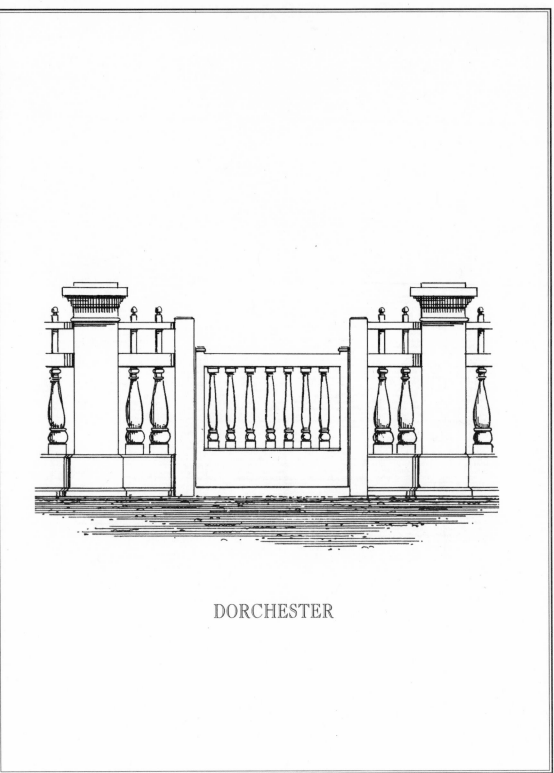

DORCHESTER

PLATE 137.

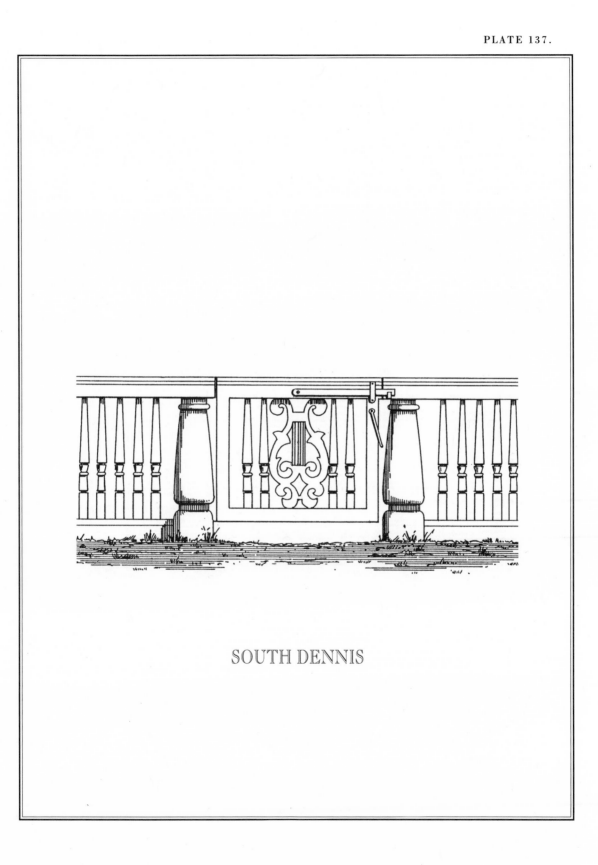

SOUTH DENNIS

PLATE 138.

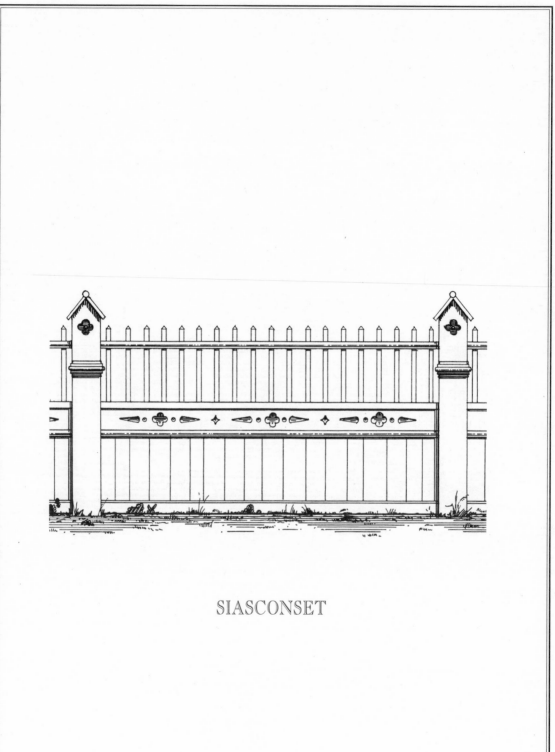

SIASCONSET

PLATE 139.

CAPE COD

PLATE 140.

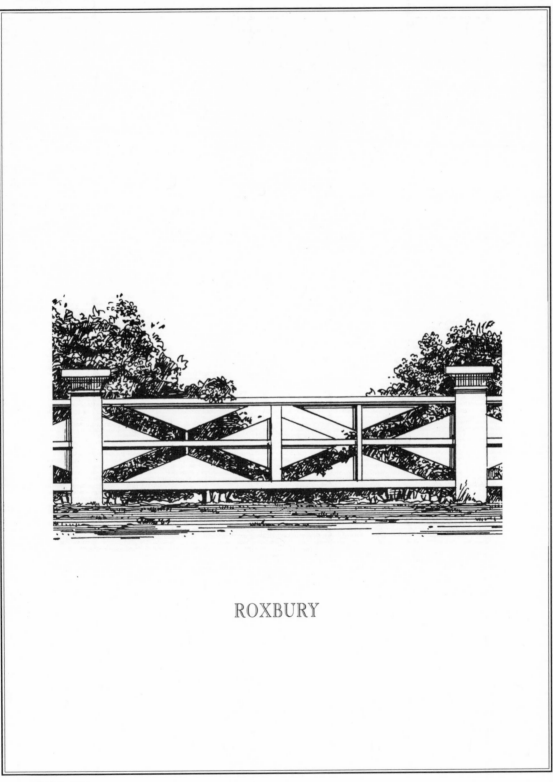

ROXBURY

PLATE 141.

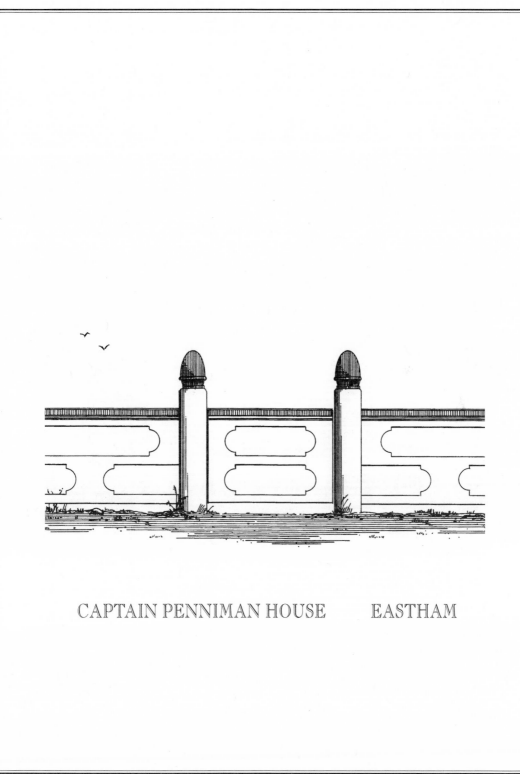

CAPTAIN PENNIMAN HOUSE     EASTHAM

PLATE 142.

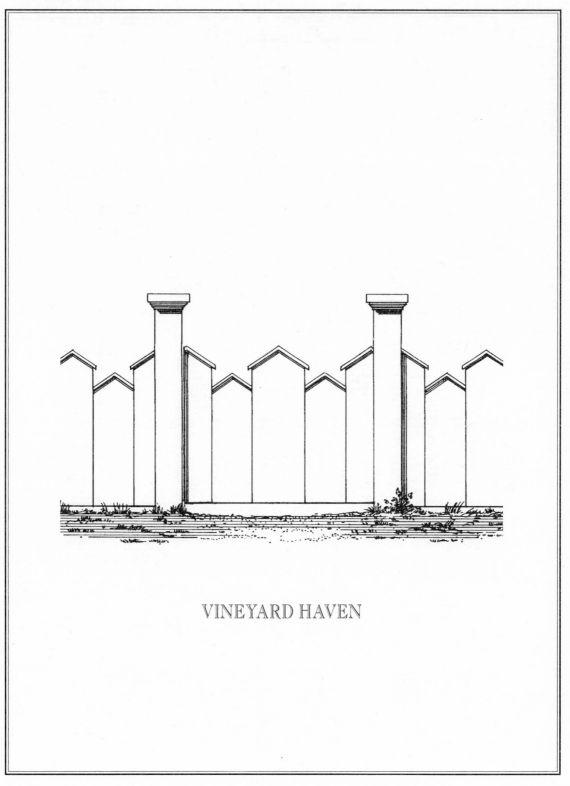

VINEYARD HAVEN

PLATE 143.

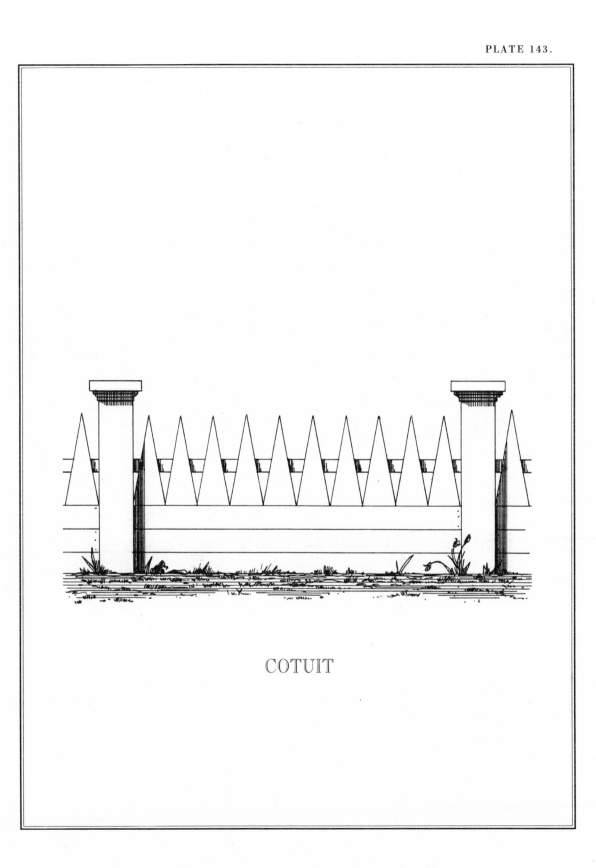

COTUIT

PLATE 144.

SIASCONSET

PLATE 145.

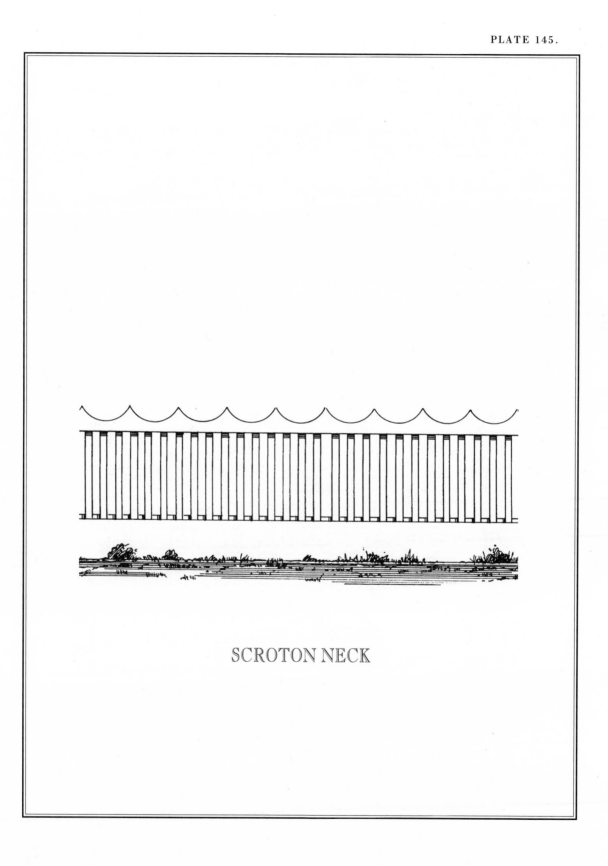

SCROTON NECK

PLATE 146.

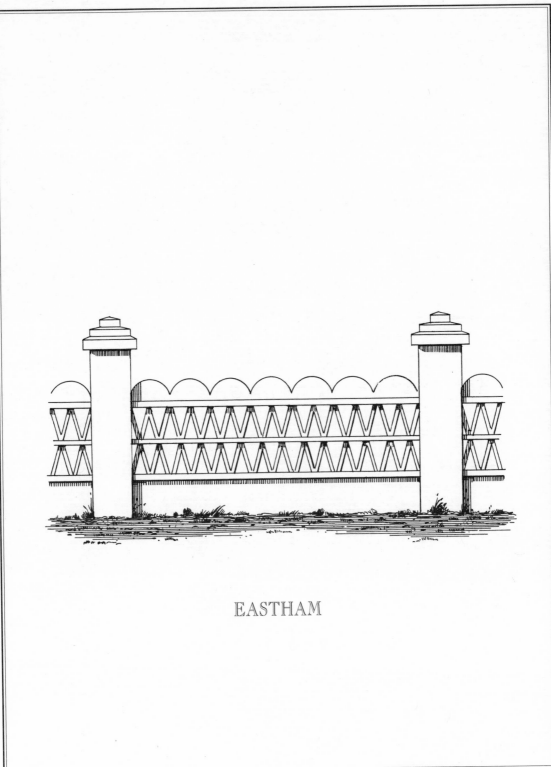

EASTHAM

# CHAPTER XVII.

―――――

## PIERS

PLATE 147.

NANTUCKET

PLATE 148.

HARWICH

PLATE 149.

KINGSTON

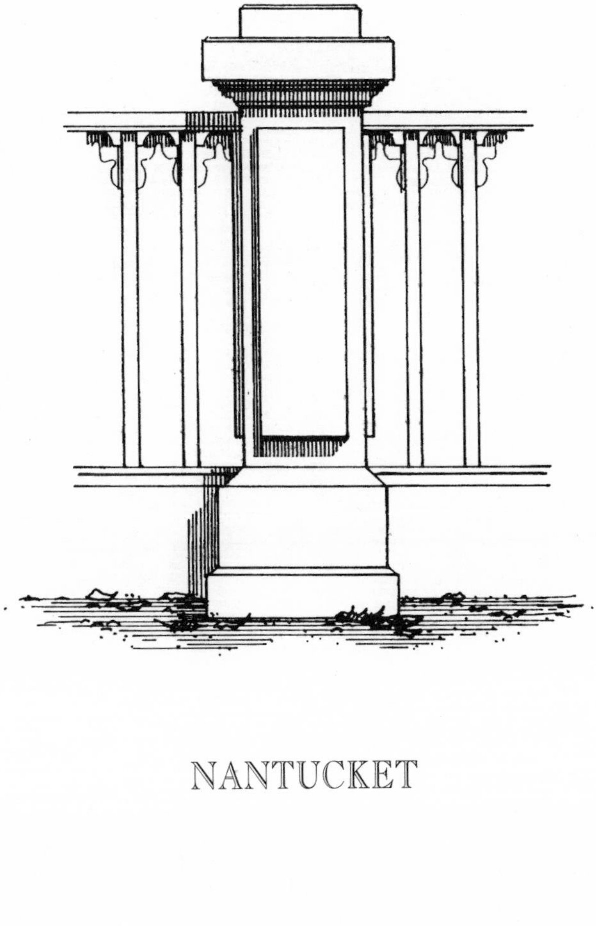

PLATE 150.

NANTUCKET

PLATE 151.

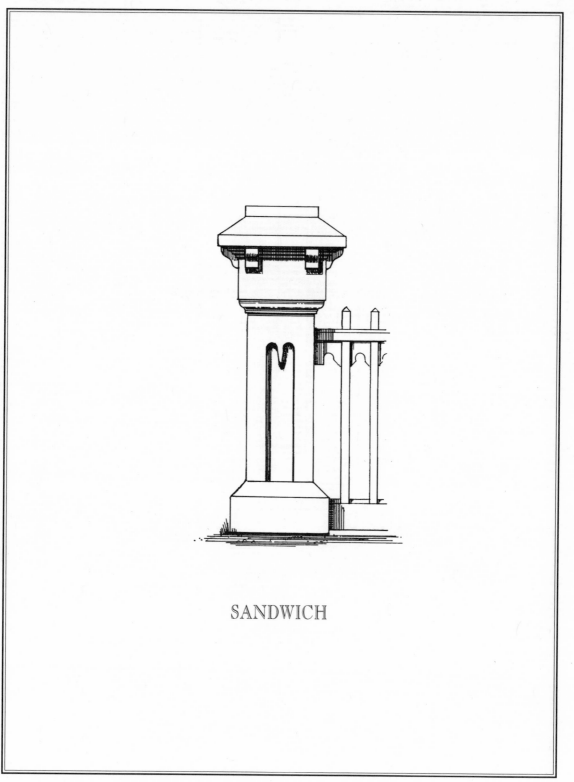

SANDWICH

PLATE 152.

SANDWICH

PLATE 153.

NANTUCKET

PLATE 154.

NANTUCKET

PLATE 155.

NANTUCKET

# CHAPTER XVIII.

---

## PICKETS

PLATE 156.

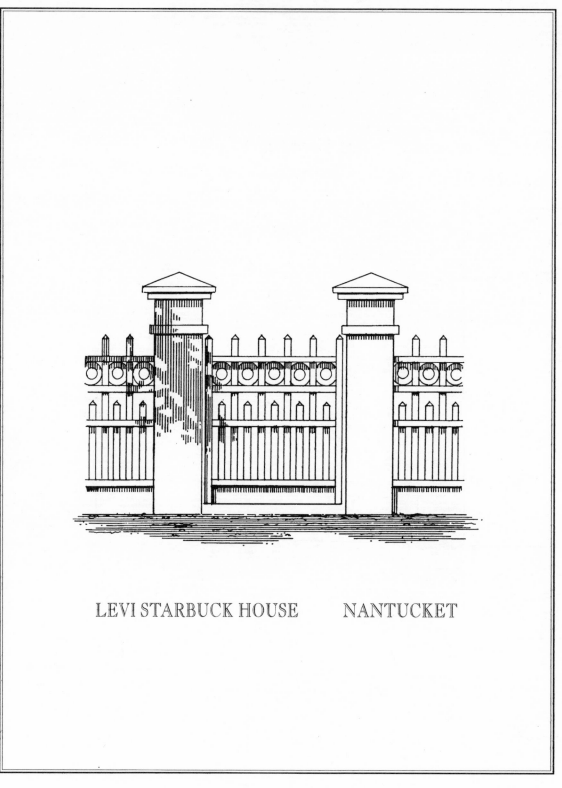

LEVI STARBUCK HOUSE     NANTUCKET

PLATE 157.

# COMMON PICKET

CAPE COD  MARTHA'S VINEYARD  YARMOUTH  YARMOUTH

PLATE 158.

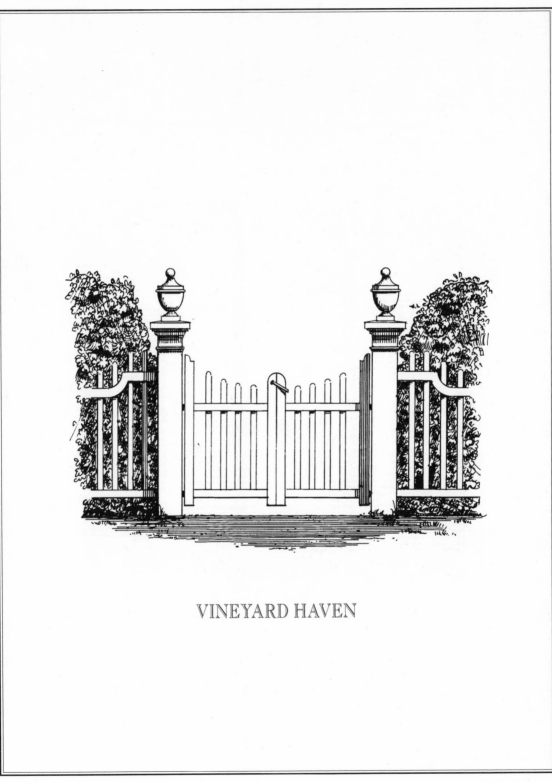

VINEYARD HAVEN

PLATE 159.

# TURNED PICKET

VINEYARD HAVEN      CENTERVILLE      NANTUCKET      FALMOUTH

PLATE 160.

FALMOUTH

PLATE 161.

# TURNED PICKET

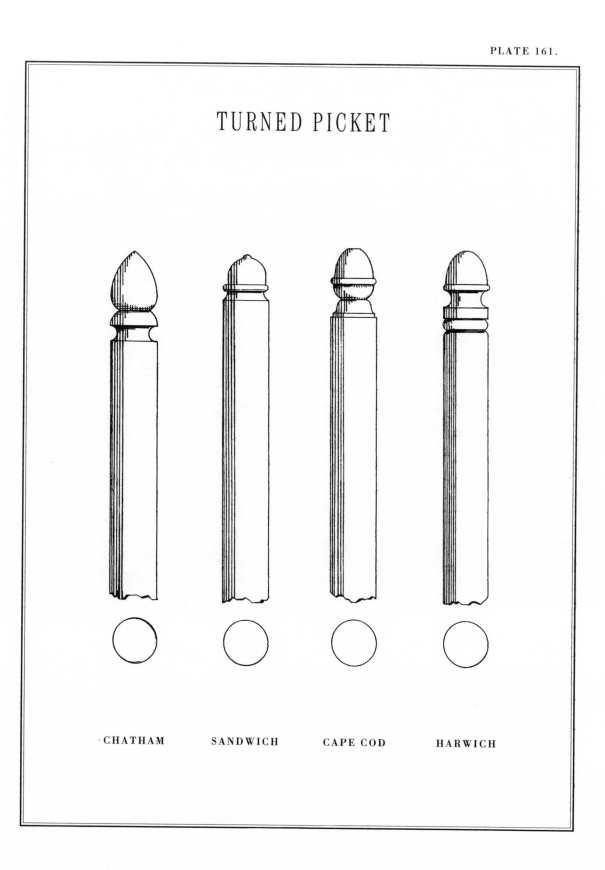

CHATHAM    SANDWICH    CAPE COD    HARWICH

PLATE 162.

NANTUCKET

# CHAPTER XIX.

---

## POLE, RAIL AND STICK FENCES

PLATE 163.

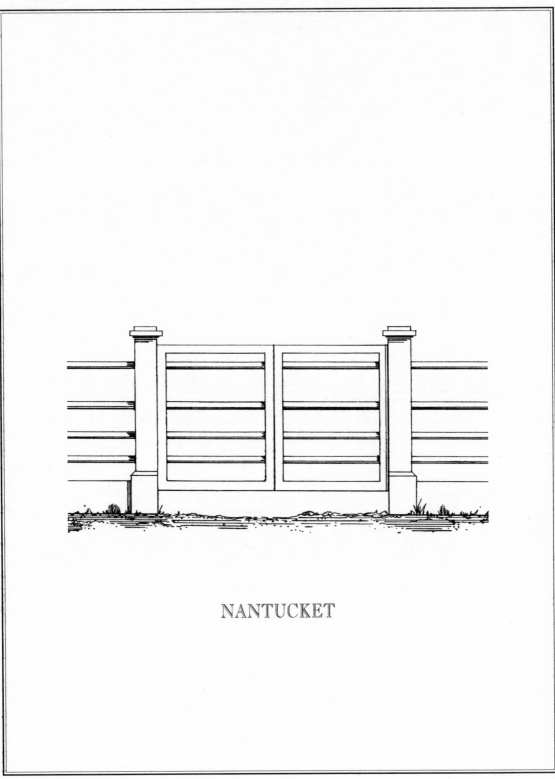

NANTUCKET

PLATE 164.

THE PETER FOLGER II HOUSE       NANTUCKET

PLATE 165.

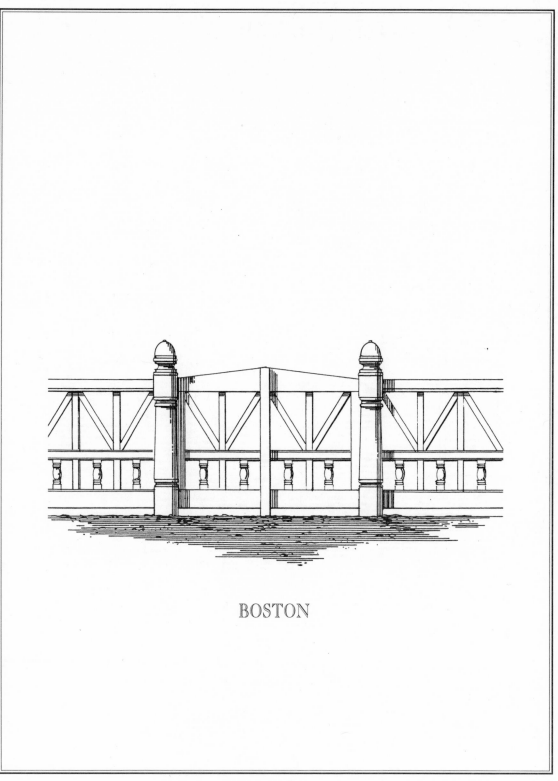

BOSTON

PLATE 166.

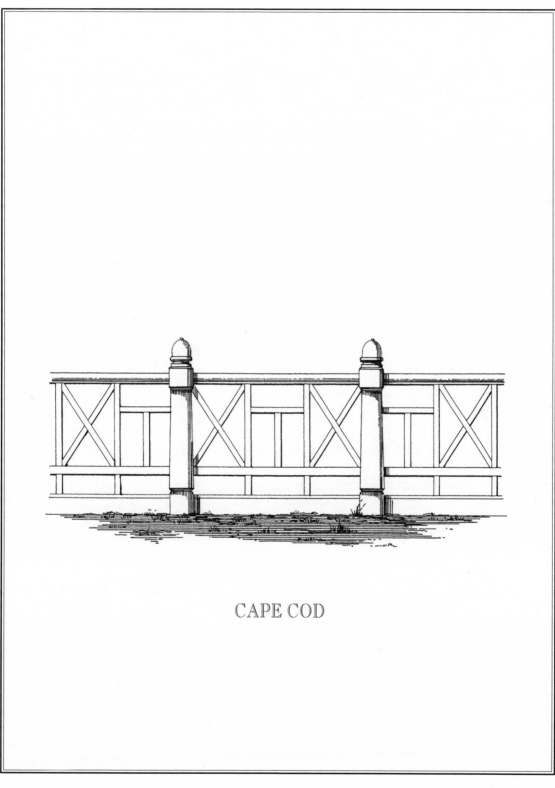

CAPE COD

PLATE 167.

FALMOUTH

PLATE 168.

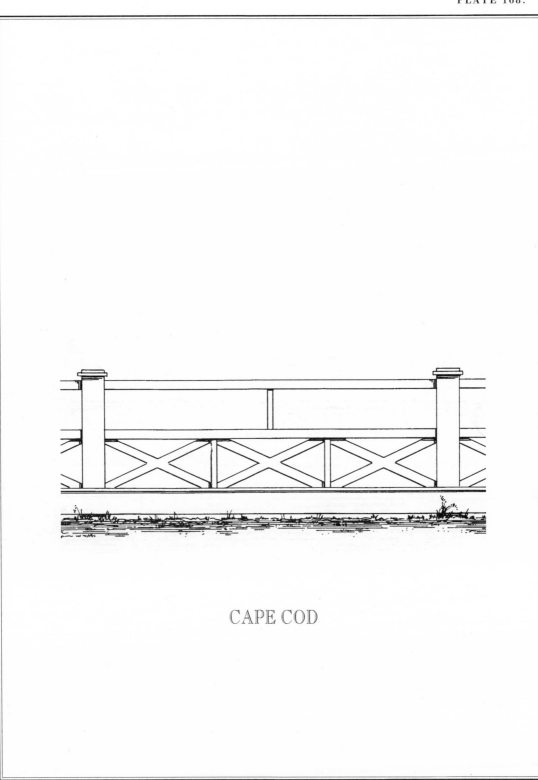

CAPE COD

PLATE 169.

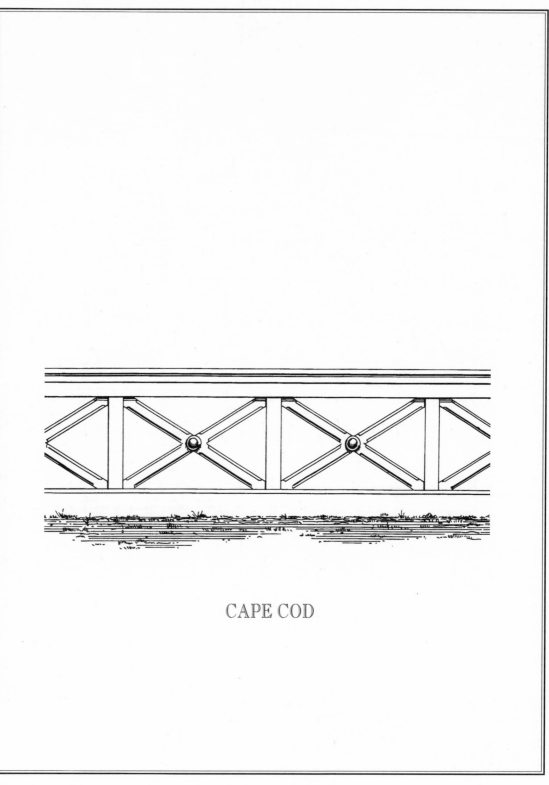

CAPE COD

# CHAPTER XX.

---

## BOARD FENCES

PLATE 170.

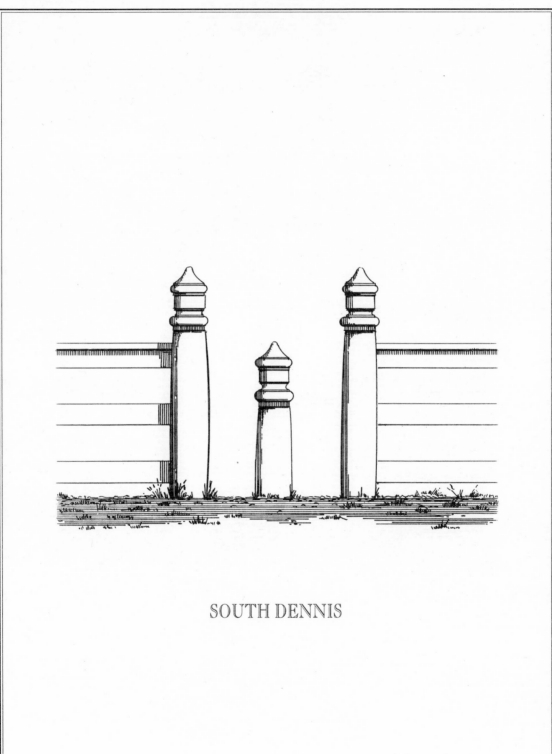

SOUTH DENNIS

PLATE 171.

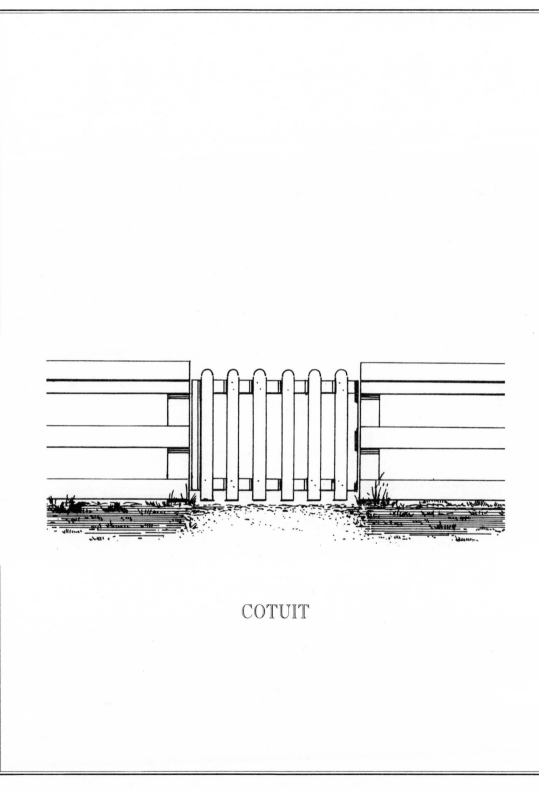

COTUIT

PLATE 172.

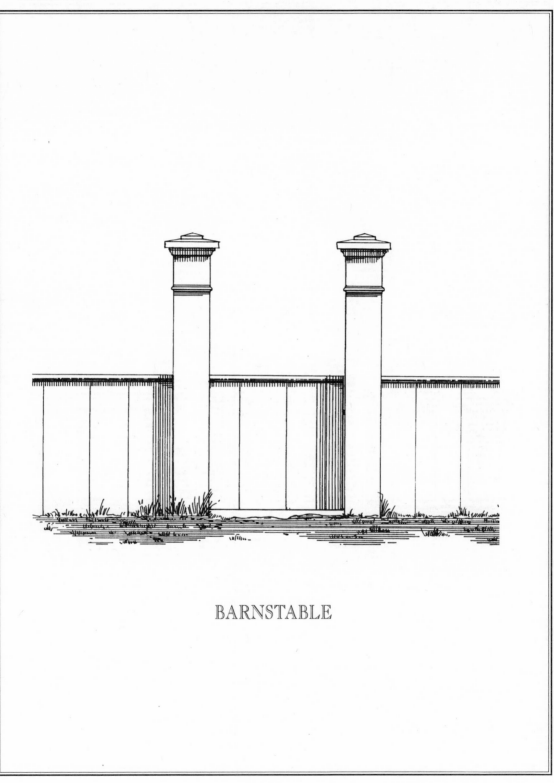

BARNSTABLE

PLATE 173.

SOUTH DENNIS

PLATE 174.

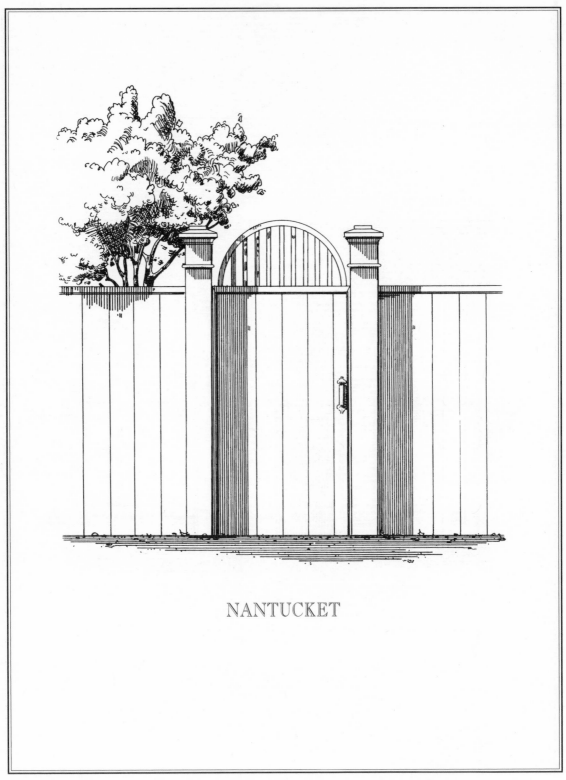

NANTUCKET

PLATE 175.

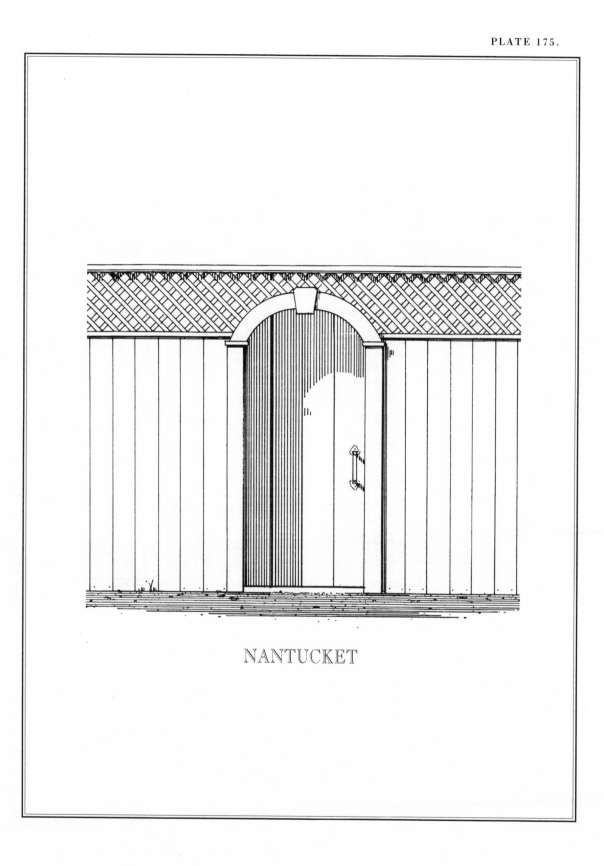

NANTUCKET

PLATE 176.

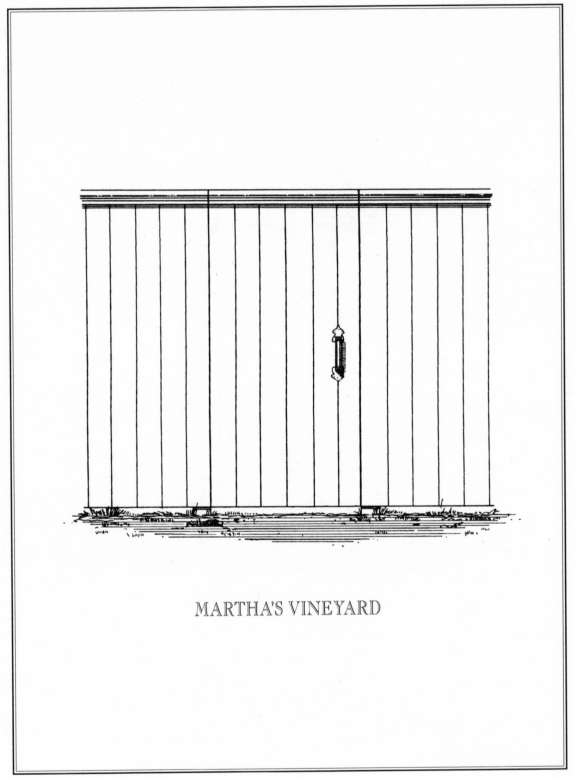

MARTHA'S VINEYARD

# CHAPTER XXI.

---

## CAPS FOR POSTS AND PIERS

PLATE 177.

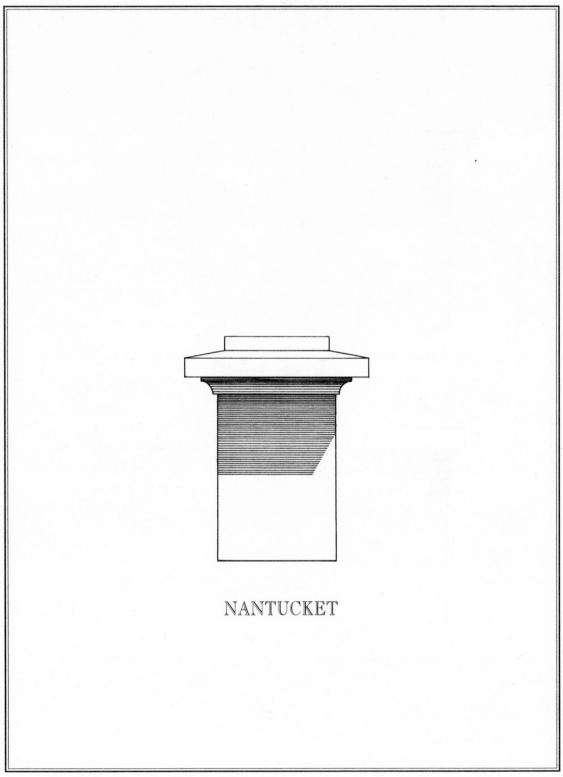

NANTUCKET

PLATE 178.

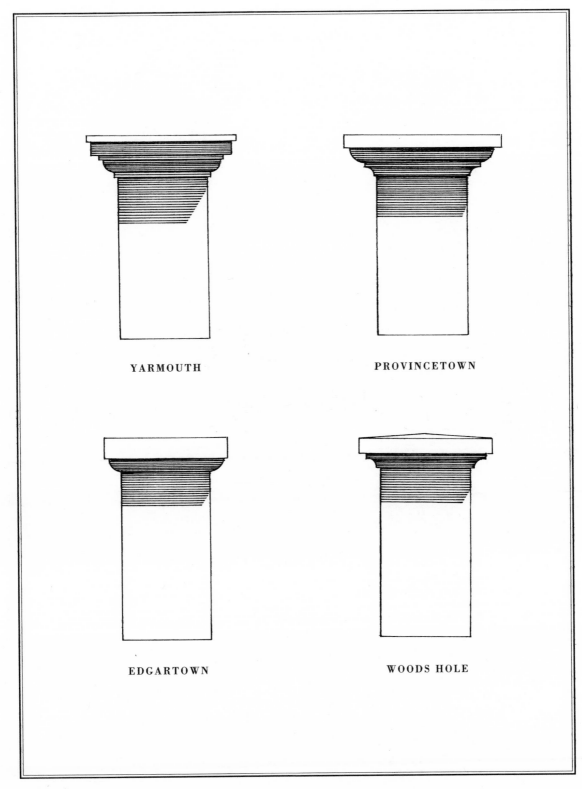

YARMOUTH

PROVINCETOWN

EDGARTOWN

WOODS HOLE

PLATE 179.

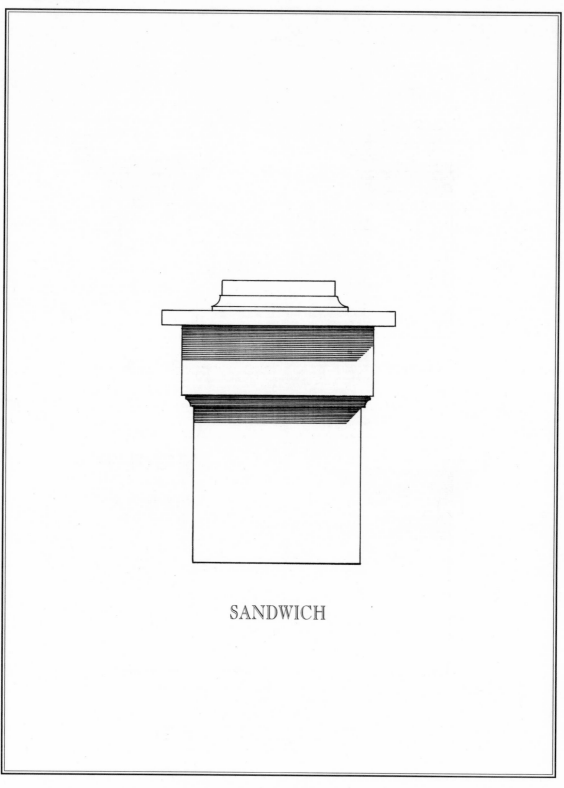

SANDWICH

PLATE 180.

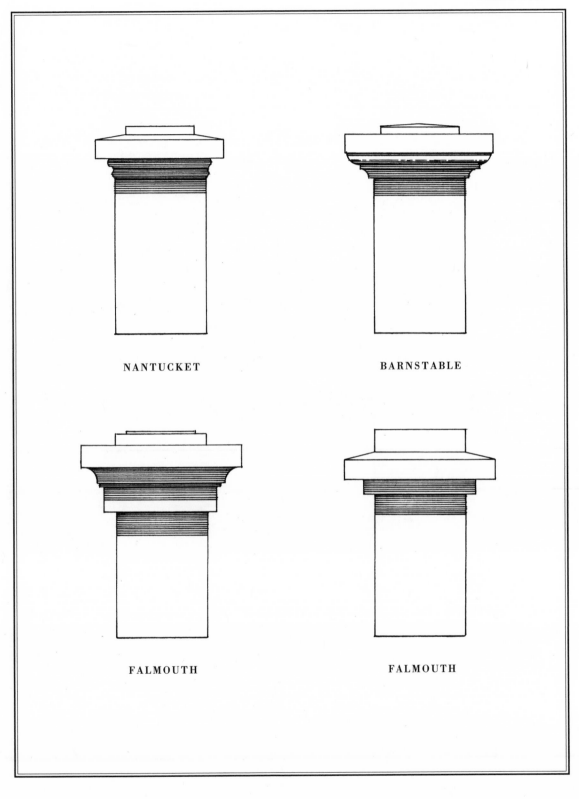

NANTUCKET

BARNSTABLE

FALMOUTH

FALMOUTH

PLATE 181.

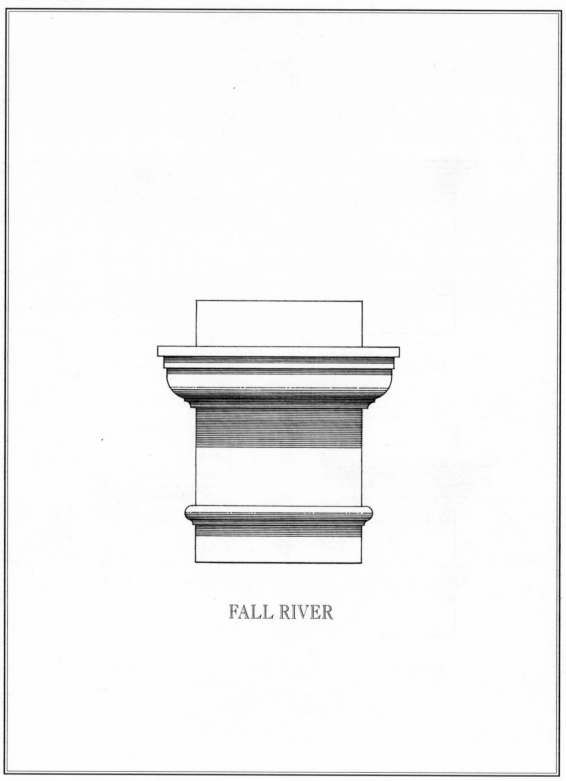

FALL RIVER

PLATE 182.

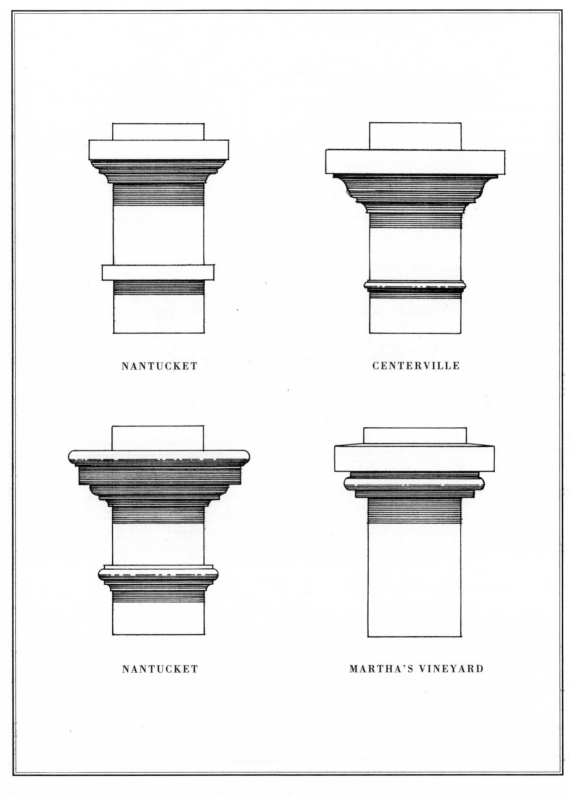

NANTUCKET

CENTERVILLE

NANTUCKET

MARTHA'S VINEYARD

PLATE 183.

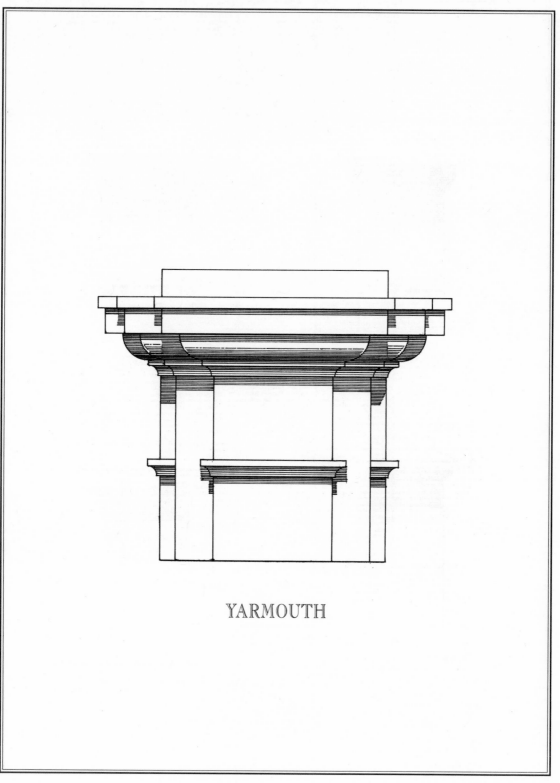

YARMOUTH

PLATE 184.

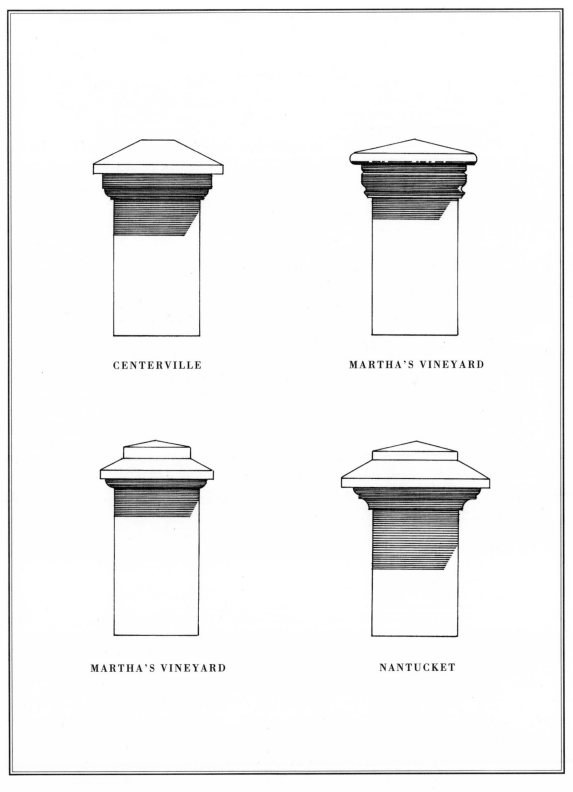

CENTERVILLE

MARTHA'S VINEYARD

MARTHA'S VINEYARD

NANTUCKET

PLATE 185.

YARMOUTH

PLATE 186.

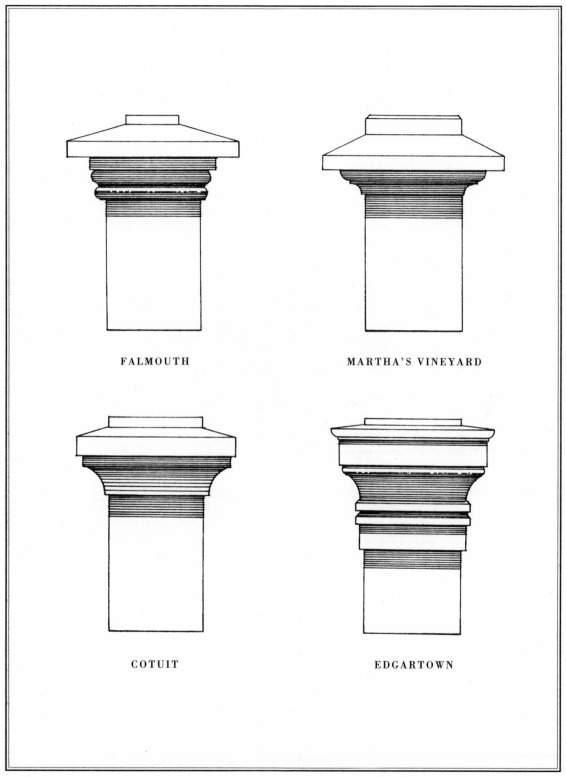

FALMOUTH

MARTHA'S VINEYARD

COTUIT

EDGARTOWN

PLATE 187.

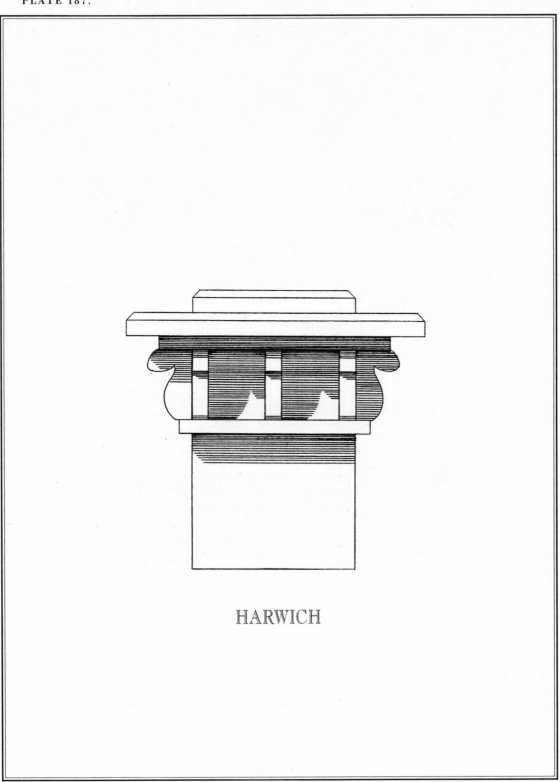

HARWICH

PLATE 188.

SANDWICH

PLATE 189.

BARNSTABLE

# CHAPTER XXII.

---

## BALLS AND URNS FOR POSTS AND PIERS

PLATE 190.

NEW BEDFORD

PLATE 191.

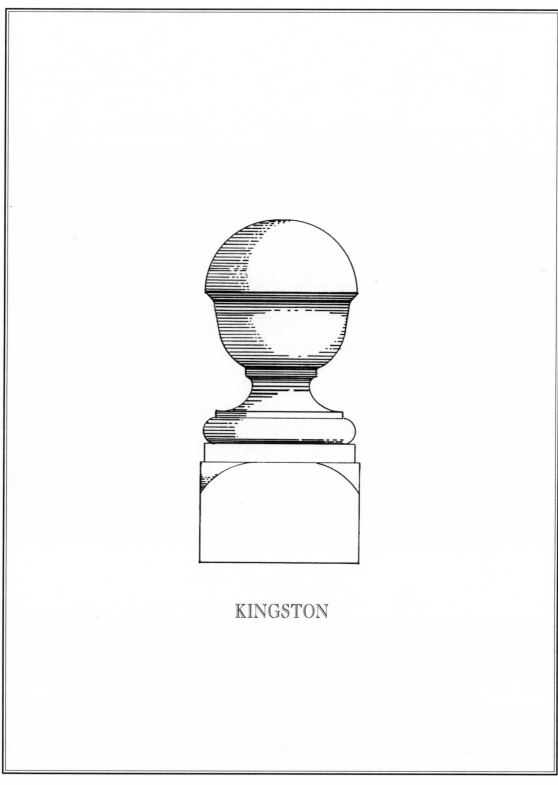

KINGSTON

PLATE 192.

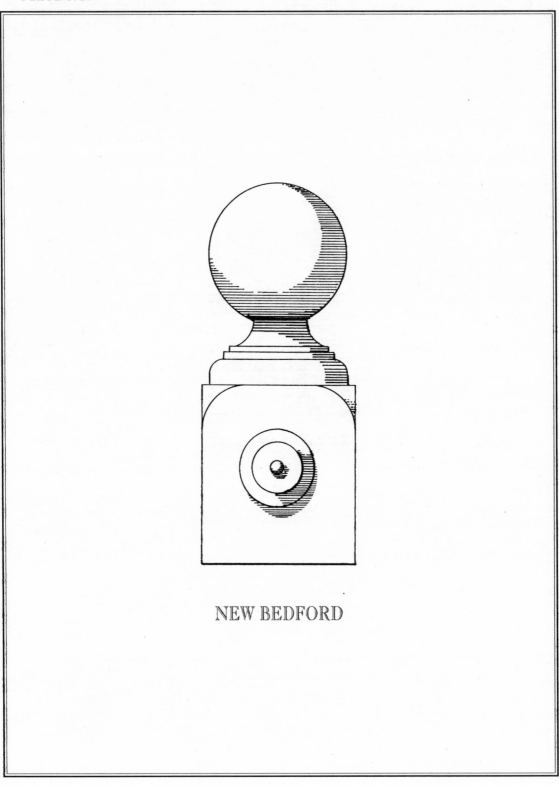

NEW BEDFORD

PLATE 193.

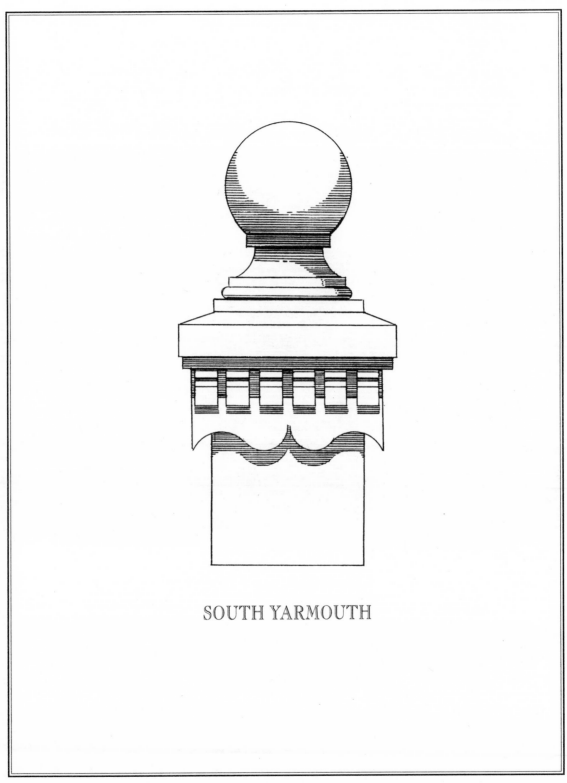

SOUTH YARMOUTH

PLATE 194.

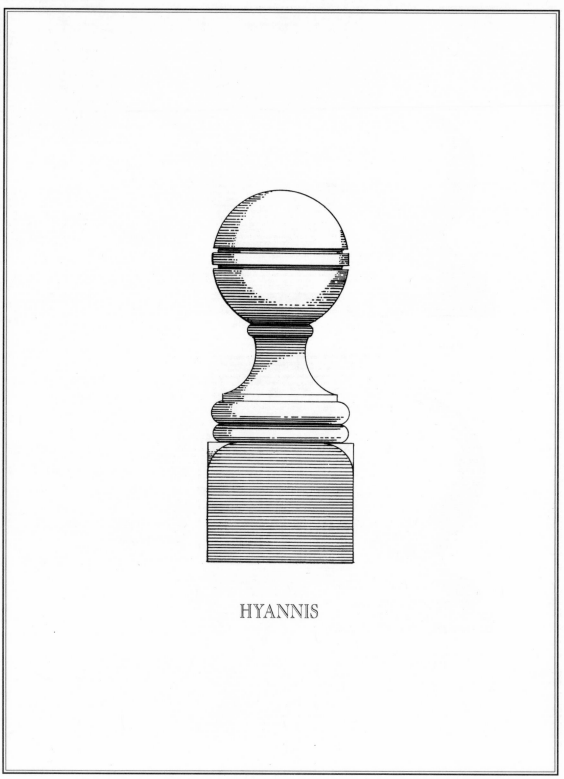

HYANNIS

PLATE 195.

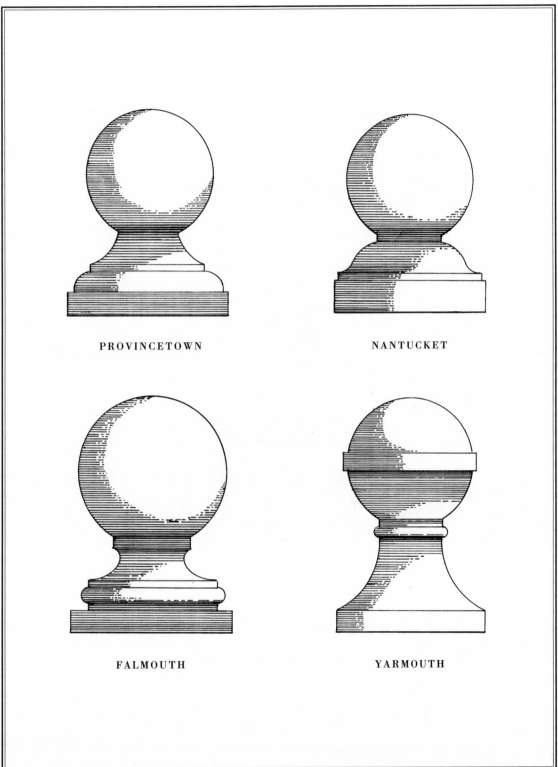

PROVINCETOWN

NANTUCKET

FALMOUTH

YARMOUTH

PLATE 196.

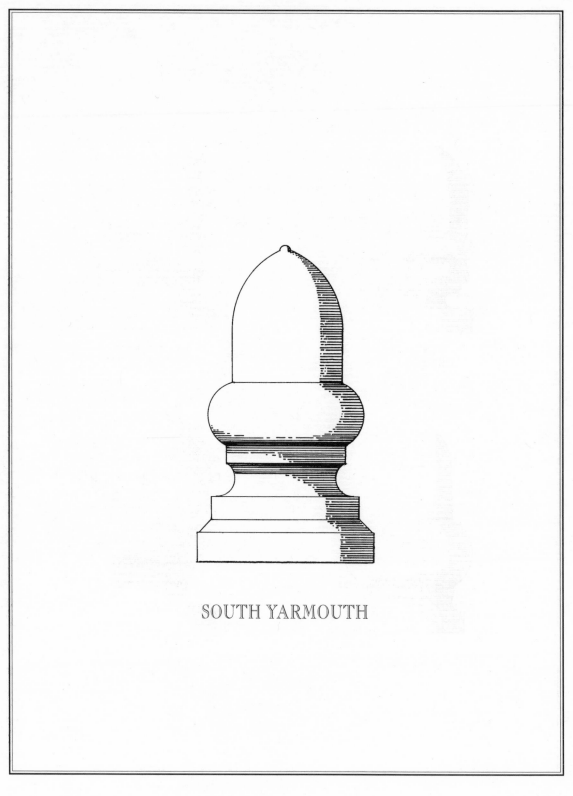

SOUTH YARMOUTH

PLATE 197.

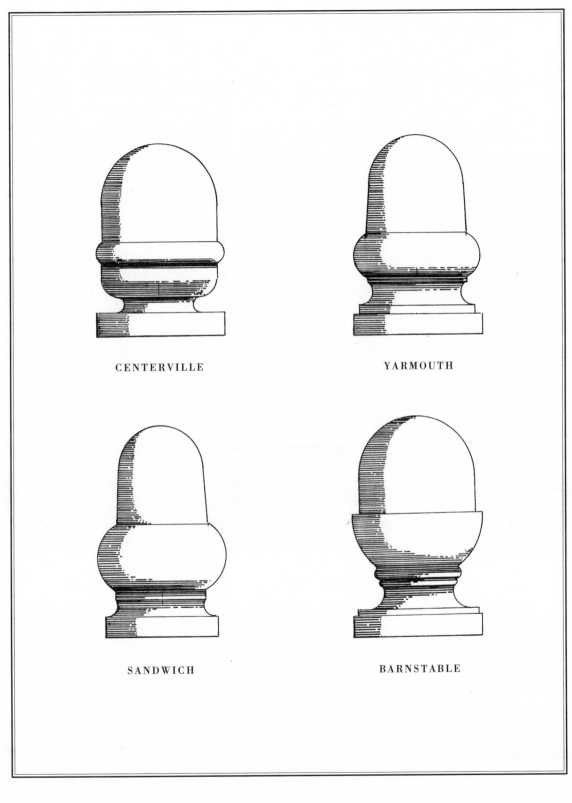

CENTERVILLE

YARMOUTH

SANDWICH

BARNSTABLE

PLATE 198.

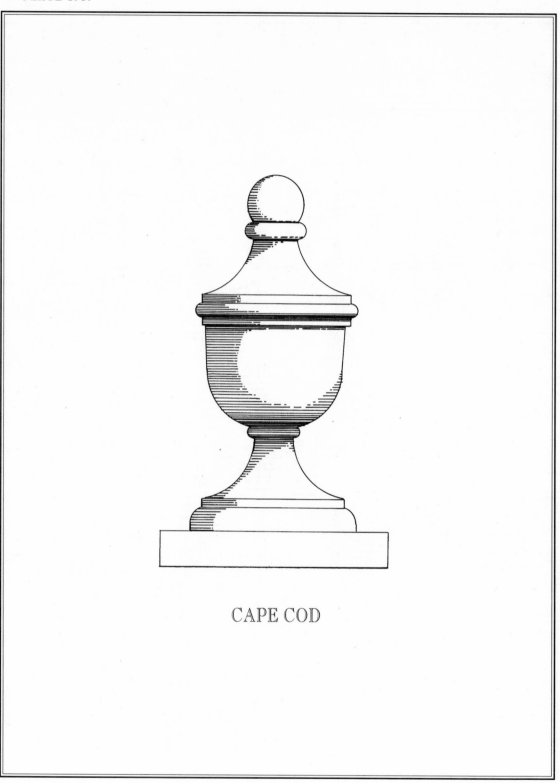

CAPE COD

PLATE 199.

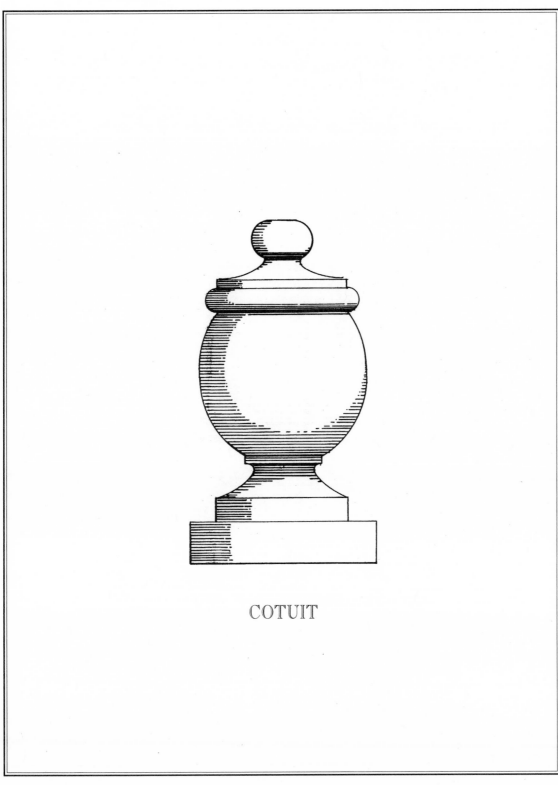

COTUIT

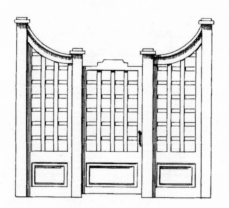

EXODUS 20:12